# The Futrell Family of East Tennessee

## The First Four Generations

Terry L. Futrell

ISBN 978-1539101062

Published by CreateSpace.com

# About the Author

Terry Futrell is a retired engineer who spends his time immersed in nature and sports photography, as well as writing an occasional newspaper feature article. The great-great-grandson of Etheldred Futrell, the first Futrell settler in East Tennessee, Terry has researched his family history for thirty years. His disciplined engineering background heavily influenced his approach to documenting family history and relationships using official records as the primary source, with little dependence on oral history or undocumented trees prepared by others. A life-long resident of Morgan and Roane Counties in Tennessee, Terry continues to live in the locale where his East Tennessee Futrell ancestors planted their roots more than 150 years ago.

# Acknowledgements

Many roadblocks were encountered during the years of genealogical research that provided the foundation for this book. Almost without exception, these roadblocks were dismantled one-by-one by Mr. Robert Bailey, Roane County Historian and Archivist. When information could not be found using traditional record sources, Robert would often disappear into his archives and surface a few minutes later with a file folder containing some obscure information that simply wasn't available from other sources. His assistance also included foraging through abandoned cemeteries in search of gravestones that might contain a key piece of information. Robert's assistance was invaluable and is very much appreciated.

Historical knowledge of the Futrell family is largely the result of three researchers, Roger H. Futrell of Kentucky, the late Morris Underwood of Texas, and Rebecca Leach Dozier of Georgia. The chapter "Early Futrell Settlers in America" would not have been possible without their decades of dedicated research.

Thanks also to Deborah Futrell Eubank whose diligence in researching the Futrell, Martin, and Ezell/Issel lines enhanced our understanding of the historical perspective of these three families. Deborah also assisted by reviewing and proofreading the book.

# Contents

# List of Figures

# Introduction

Imagine finding out that your great-great-grandfather obtained two marriage licenses on the same day!

Imagine browsing through your great-great-grandfather's military records at the U.S. National Archives and discovering that he was charged with desertion from the Union Army!

Imagine answering your doorbell to find a California stranger bringing your great-grandfather's family Bible and Civil War discharge certificate to give to you!

These are just three of the many surprises encountered during thirty years of researching the origins of my East Tennessee Futrell family. It has been a long and arduous search, and false assumptions and misinformation have led the research down many wrong pathways. Even after thirty years, it was still not possible to connect the East Tennessee Futrells to their ancestors in North Carolina, leaving a gaping hole in the family tree. Finally, after obtaining a DNA analysis a few months ago, the gap began to close. Though not providing an answer with absolute certainty, the DNA evidence suggests that the gap is now closed.

The following information provides a summary of research on the East Tennessee Futrells who were initially located in Knox County and later migrated to Roane and Morgan Counties. First, background is provided on the early Futrell settlers in America. Then, the migration of great-great-grandfather Etheldred Futrell from North Carolina to Knox County, Tennessee, and eventually to Roane County, and then Morgan County, is presented. Lastly, each of the Etheldred Futrell descendants is documented through the fourth generation. Sources are provided for all information to establish the validity of the family relationships.

Throughout their history in America, the Futrell name has been pronounced in various ways. Because many early Futrells could not read or write, the spelling in official records was typically based on how the person filling out the record thought the name should be spelled. Consequently, there are many variations in spelling in the official records. In such cases, the name is typically presented in this book as it was spelled in the official record.

Due to reliance primarily on official sources, it is possible that some descendants have been omitted. As an example, a child that was born and died between censuses would potentially be missed. Unless these were identified through family Bible records or burial records, they are not included.

# Early Futrell Settlers in America

*Thomas Futrell I was born in England about
1658/59 and died in Surry County VA
shortly before 11 April 1693. He was, I
believe, the progenitor of the Futrell Family
in America.*

— Morris Underwood[1]

According to the research of Morris Underwood,
"Although no specific record of the date has been found
Thomas Futrell I, based on other available records, arrived
in the Virginia Colony sometime in 1676 in the company of
Mr. Robert Ruffin."[2] Since the date of Underwood's work, a
passenger list has been published that indicates Futerell
came to America in 1679.[3] Thomas Futerell was brought to
the Virginia Colony as an indentured servant by Robert
Ruffin, whose estate was located in the Jamestown
settlement of Surry County and who claimed a headright
(50-acre land patent) for bringing Thomas to the Colony.
Surry County lay south of the James River and ran to the
North Carolina border. Futerell was judged by the Surry
County Court to be eighteen years old on 16 September

---

[1] Morris Underwood, A Chronology of Public Records of Interest for
Thomas Futrell I of Surry County, Virginia and Thomas Futrell II of
Northampton County, North Carolina, (Unpublished Work, 1999), 56
[2] Underwood, *Chronology*, 14
[3] Ancestry.com, U.S. and Canada, Passenger and Immigration Lists
Index, 1500s-1900s, (Ancestry.com Operations, Inc., 2010), 204

1677.[4] This judgment should not be construed to indicate that Futerell's age was 18, but that, after release from his indenture, he was at least 18 years old and subject to paying tax to the colony.

When Thomas Futerell completed his indenture with Robert Ruffin he married a widow, Mrs. Jillian Alderson, in 1684. Futerell died in 1693 and his wife was appointed administrator of his estate on 28 April 1693 in Surry County. Futerell apparently left behind two sons, William, who died 15 January 1726/1727 in Virginia, and Thomas II, who settled in North Carolina by 1720.[5]

> *Researchers have consistently assumed that the elder Thomas Futrell of Northampton County, North Carolina, was the son of Thomas Futerell of Surry County, Virginia. Compelling circumstantial evidence suggests that they were father and son, but to date no primary documentation has surfaced to prove their relationship, however, no other Futrells lived in the Surry County, Virginia-Chowan Precinct, North Carolina, region at the time.[6]*

Thomas Futrell II migrated south to the North Carolina colony where he was the only Futrell listed in the public records of North Carolina before 1735. He first

---

[4] Roger H. Futrell, *The Futrell Family Revised*, (Unpublished Work, 2009), 4
[5] Futrell, *Futrell Family Revised*, 8
[6] Futrell, *Futrell Family Revised*, 8

appeared in court records for the Chowan Precinct of Albemarle County, in the Carolina Colony, in 1720.[7]

> *Thomas Futrell [of Northampton] was the father of five sons and the ancestor of all Futrells I have found across the United States. Records show there is no other Futrell in the area old enough to be the sons' father except Thomas. The sons included Joseph, Thomas, Jr., John, Benjamin and William. Thomas Futrell, II and most of his five sons had grist mills.[8]*
> — Rev. Norman J. Flythe

The nationwide 1790 United States Census schedules reveal that all Futrills lived in the same rural community of Northampton County, NC, except for Moore Feutral who lived in nearby Onslow County.

Benjamin Futrell, son of Thomas II and Ann (surname unknown) Futrell, was born around 1715, either in Surry County, Virginia, or in North Carolina. Benjamin died before June 1790, leaving a will written 26 October 1784 that was probated in June court 1790, Northampton County, North Carolina. Benjamin mentioned the following children in his will: Elizabeth Mainer, Mary Bagby, Milla Futrell, Thomas, Benjamin, Jr., Arthur, Frederick, Moore, and Etheldred [not the Etheldred who later migrated to

---

[7] Futrell, *Futrell Family Revised*, 12
[8] Futrell, *Futrell Family Revised*, 13

Tennessee].[9] Apparently, Etheldred was the eldest because his father's plantation was left to him. Benjamin's son, Moore Futrell migrated to Onslow County, North Carolina before 1790.[10]

[9] Rebecca Leach Dozier, *Twelve Northampton County, North Carolina Families 1650-1850*, (Baltimore: Gateway Press, Inc., 2004), 140
[10] Ancestry.com, *1790 United States Federal Census*, Ancestry.com Operations, Inc:2010, Year: 1790; Census Place: Onslow, North Carolina; Series: M637; Roll: 7; Page: 4; Image: 353; Family History Library Film: 0568147

# Futrell Migration

To fully understand the beginnings of the East Tennessee Futrells, one must consider the relationships among three families, headed by John B. Walls, John Martin, and Etheldred Futrell, and their migration. All three of these men were born in North Carolina and initially migrated to Knox County, Tennessee.

Both John Martin and John B. Walls migrated to Tennessee at a relatively young age. John Martin, born in 1791, married Nancy Issel in Knox County, Tennessee, on 28 December 1808 at the age of 17.[11] John B. Walls, born in 1795, married Anna Wolf in Knox County, Tennessee, on 21 May 1822 at the age of 27.[12] The two families apparently lived in the same Knox County community as Samuel Martin, son of John Martin, married Charlotte Charity Walls, daughter of John B. Walls, on 25 November 1841 in Knox County.[13]

The first official record bringing Etheldred Futrell into this familial relationship is his marriage to Sarah Martin Nichodemus, the previously married daughter of

---

[11] Yates Publishing. *U.S. and International Marriage Records, 1560-1900* [database on-line]. Provo, UT, USA: Ancestry.com Operations Inc, 2004.
[12] Ancestry.com, *Tennessee State Marriages, 1780-2002*, Online publication - Provo, UT, USA: Ancestry.com Operations Inc, 2008
[13] Ancestry.com, Tennessee State Marriages, 1780-2002

John and Nancy Issel Martin, on 19 September 1837 in Knox County.[14] Based on the date of his birth calculated from his age at death listed on his gravestone, Etheldred Futrell would have been 37 years old at the time of his marriage to Sarah. All three men – John Martin, John B. Walls, and Etheldred Futrell – were separated in age by no more than nine years.

While the parents of these three men and their North Carolina place of birth have not been proven, recent DNA testing of their descendants provides some clues that provide a basis for future genealogical research. DNA testing has revealed with an extremely high confidence level that descendants of William Madison Wall, son of Isaac Wall of Rockingham County, North Carolina, are cousins to descendants of John B. Walls.[15] Twenty-nine families having the surname Martin also lived in Rockingham County in 1820[16], and ten families having the surname Martin lived across the state line in Henry County, Virginia, wherein lies the town of Martinsville.[17] It is possible that the families of John Martin and John B.

---

[14] Ancestry.com, Tennessee State Marriages, 1780-2002
[15] Ancestry.com, DNA Matches for Terry Futrell
[16] Ancestry.com, *1820 United States Federal Census*, Ancestry.com Operations, Inc:2010, **Year: 1820; Census Place: Rockingham County, North Carolina; Series: M33**
[17] Ancestry.com, *1820 United States Federal Census*, Ancestry.com Operations, Inc:2010, **Year: 1820; Census Place: Henry, Virginia; Series: M33**

Walls migrated together from North Carolina to Knox County, Tennessee.

DNA testing also revealed that Moore Futrell of Onslow County, North Carolina, was likely the father of Etheldred Futrell who migrated to Knox County, Tennessee.[18] It appears likely that Etheldred Futrell migrated from Onslow County to Knox County much later than the migration of John Martin and John B. Walls, as no record has been found that places him in Tennessee before his marriage in 1837.

Family lore, as expressed by an Etheldred Futrell great-grandson in 1994, held that Etheldred was a sea captain before coming to Tennessee.[19] It is interesting to note that Onslow County, North Carolina, is located on the Atlantic Coast and was a prominent shipbuilding center in the early 1800s[20]. It is possible that Etheldred spent his early years at sea, thereby accounting for his migration to Tennessee and marriage when in his late thirties.

It is also interesting to note that several Ezell families lived in Duplin County where Moore Futrell resided during Etheldred's childhood.[21] "Issel", the maiden

---

[18] Ancestry.com, DNA Matches for Terry Futrell
[19] Personal interview with Lewis L. Futrell, 1994
[20] http://www.northcarolinahistory.org/encyclopedia/611/entry/
[21] Ancestry.com. *North Carolina, Compiled Census and Census Substitutes Index, 1790-1890* [database on-line]. Provo, UT, USA: Ancestry.com Operations Inc, 1999.

name of John Martin's wife, Nancy, was often used as a variant of "Ezell". It is possible that Etheldred Futrell's initial connection to John Martin came through a relationship between the Futrell and Ezell families in North Carolina.

# Generation 1: Etheldred Futrell, Progenitor of the East Tennessee Futrells

**1.0 Etheldred Futrell** was born 1 August 1800[22] in North Carolina.[23] While his father has not been proven, DNA testing of descendants shows with a high confidence level that Etheldred was the son of Moore Futrell who lived in Onslow County.[24] Note that the 1800 census shows Moore Futrell living in adjoining Duplin County, North Carolina, but he was once again in Onslow County in the 1810 census.

Etheldred first appeared in official records in Tennessee when he married Sarah Martin Nichodemus, the previously married daughter of John and Nancy Issel Martin, in Knox County on 19 September 1837.[25] Two marriage licenses are listed in records with the same date. One lists Sarah as Sarah Martin, and the second lists her as Sarah Nichodemus. Other records show that Sarah was

---

[22] Date calculated from age and date of death listed on gravestone (83 yr, 7 mo, 28 days, died 29 March 1884)
[23] Ancestry.com, *1850 United States Federal Census*, Ancestry.com Operations, Inc:2009, Year: 1850; Census Place: Knoxville, Knox, Tennessee; Roll: M432_886; Page: 107A; Image: 215
[24] Ancestry.com, DNA Matches for Terry Futrell
[25] Ancestry.com, Tennessee State Marriages, 1780-2002

previously married to Frederick Nichodemus in Knox County on 14 September 1831.[26]

The 1850 census shows Etheldred in the town of Knoxville in Knox County as head of household with his occupation listed as shoe making.[27] His in-laws, John and Nancy Martin, are living in the same household, as well as the two children of Etheldred and Sarah, Mary (age 7) and John (age 4). Also listed within the household is Samuel Lawless (age 6), the apparent son of Sarah's sister Melinda and her husband Jesse Lawless.

Apparently, Sarah Futrell died shortly after the 1850 census was taken. Also, Melinda Martin Lawless and her husband Jesse apparently divorced around 1850. This occurred after the conception of their son James, shown as age 0 in the 1850 census, which lists Melinda Lawless as head of household.[28] James' death record indicates his date of birth as 4 November 1850.[29] After Sarah's death, Etheldred Futrell married his sister-in-law Melinda Martin Lawless on 20 May 1851 in Knox County.[30]

---

[26] Ancestry.com, Tennessee State Marriages, 1780-2002
[27] Ancestry.com, *1850 United States Federal Census*, Ancestry.com Operations, Inc:2009, Year: 1850; Census Place: Knoxville, Knox, Tennessee; Roll: M432_886; Page: 107A; Image: 215
[28] Ancestry.com, *1850 United States Federal Census*, Ancestry.com Operations, Inc:2009, Year: 1850; Census Place: Subdivision 15, Knox, Tennessee; Roll: M432_886; Page: 177B; Image: 356
[29] Ancestry.com, *Tennessee Death Records, 1908-1958*, Ancestry.com Operations, Inc:2011, Tennessee State Library and Archives; Nashville, Tennessee; Tennessee Death Records, 1908-1959; Roll #: 10
[30] Ancestry.com, Tennessee State Marriages, 1780-2002

Etheldred and Melinda later had a son, Noah, born in March 1852.[31]

At some time between 1851 and 1860, the Futrell, Martin, and Walls families moved from Knox County to Roane and Morgan Counties in Tennessee.

The 1860 census shows Etheldred as head of household living in District 14 of Roane County having the Webster post office.[32] Etheldred's occupation was listed as shoe and boot maker. Also living in the household were his wife Melinda, his children Mary A., John, and Noah, and three of Melinda's children by her former marriage, Nancy J., Pam, and James Lawless (Golis in the census document). Based on the families listed nearby in the census, the Futrell family was most likely located in the vicinity of the current Big Emory Baptist Church. Melinda's son William Lawless (Lollis) and daughter-in-law Margaret Bennett Futrell are buried in the Webster Cemetery behind the church.

---

[31] Ancestry.com, *1900 United States Federal Census*, Ancestry.com Operations, Inc:2004, Year: 1900; Census Place: Civil District 14, Roane, Tennessee; Roll: 1593; Page: 19B; Enumeration District: 0116; FHL microfilm: 1241593

[32] Ancestry.com, *1860 United States Federal Census*, Ancestry.com Operations, Inc:2009, Year: 1860; Census Place: District 14, Roane, Tennessee; Roll: M653_1269; Page: 228; Image: 466; Family History Library Film: 805269

**Evidence that Moore Futrell was the father of Etheldred Futrell who migrated to East Tennessee**

1. A comparison of the DNA of a great-great-grandson of Etheldred Futrell of Morgan County, performed by Ancestry.com, identified eight other Futrell descendants who are projected to be fourth cousins – six of these cousins are direct descendants of Moore Futrell.
2. DNA results reveal 13 Futrell cousins for which the confidence level of the analysis is extremely high, very high, or high. Twelve are known to be direct descendants of Moore Futrell.
3. The possible range of the relationship to other Futrell cousins established by DNA analysis indicates an extremely high probability that one of the sons of Benjamin Futrell was the father of Etheldred Futrell of Morgan County.
4. An analysis of North Carolina census records for Moore Futrell reveals that he had at least one son of the age of Etheldred Futrell that previously has not been accounted for by Futrell family researchers.

**Evidence that Etheldred Futrell of East Tennessee was not Etheldred Futrell, Jr. of Johnston County, North Carolina**

Many researchers have erroneously assumed Etheldred Futrell of Morgan County as Etheldred Futrell, Jr., son of Etheldred Futrell, Sr. of Johnston County, North Carolina. Etheldred Sr. was the brother of Moore Futrell. Undisputable evidence disproves this:

1. Etheldred Futrell, Jr. married Edna "Edney" Gearold in Johnston County on 2 July 1821. The 1850 census shows them living in Desoto County, Mississippi next door to their daughter Martha and her husband J.P. Walton.
2. The obituary of Martha Futrell Walton published in the Nashville Christian Advocate on January 16, 1886 clearly identifies Martha as the daughter of Etheldred and Edna Futrell and states that she was born in Johnson [sic] County, North Carolina.

Apparently John Martin died before 1860, either before or after the migration, because his wife Nancy is shown in the household of her son Samuel Martin and his wife Charlotte Charity Walls Martin in the 1860 census living in District 14 of Roane County having the Olivers post office.[33]

The 1860 census shows John B. Walls living a few miles away from the other families across Walden Ridge in District 1 of Morgan County having the Crooked Fork post office.[34]

Etheldred Futrell, together with his son John and several other Roane and Morgan County men traveled to Flat Lick, Kentucky, where they enlisted in the Union Army on 10 February 1862.[35] Etheldred's stepsons, William and Samuel Lawless, had enlisted in the 1st Regiment Tennessee Infantry six months earlier in 1861.[36] Etheldred was 62 years old at the time of his enlistment in

[33] Ancestry.com, *1860 United States Federal Census*, Ancestry.com Operations, Inc:2009, Year: 1860; Census Place: District 14, Roane, Tennessee; Roll: M653_1269; Page: 234; Image: 478; Family History Library Film: 805269

[34] Ancestry.com, *1860 United States Federal Census*, Ancestry.com Operations, Inc:2009, Year: 1860; Census Place: District 1, Morgan, Tennessee; Roll: M653_1266; Page: 478; Image: 309; Family History Library Film: 805266

[35] www.fold3.com, *Page 1 Civil War Soldiers - Union - TN - Fold3*, https://www.fold3.com/image/267068122/?xid=1022

[36] Ancestry.com Ancestry.com, *U.S., Union Soldiers Compiled Service Records, 1861-1865*, Ancestry.com Operations, Inc:2011

Company H, 3rd Regiment of the Tennessee Infantry Volunteers.

A few months after his enlistment, Etheldred was captured at the Battle of London, Kentucky, on 17 August 1862 by the Kirby Smith Brigade of the First Louisiana Cavalry under the command of Colonel John S. Scott.[37] The Confederates captured "120 men, 100 wagons and over 400 horses and mules."[38] Due to his age and ill health, Etheldred was released in December of 1862 and returned home. Not knowing that he had been captured, Etheldred was charged with desertion by the Union Army. This wasn't known by the family until his death on 29 March 1884 when a military gravestone was requested. A search of military records revealed his capture by the Confederates and the charge of desertion was removed from his record.[39] A military gravestone was then provided for his grave in the Ritter Cemetery in the Coalhill community of Morgan County.

Etheldred and Melinda Futrell were shown living alone in District 16 of Roane County in the 1870 census near their son Noah and near Melinda's son James

---

[37] www.fold3.com, *Page 1 Civil War Soldiers - Union - TN - Fold3*, https://www.fold3.com/image/267068122/?xid=1022
[38] Facebook, 1st Louisiana Cavalry Regiment, CSA
[39] www.fold3.com, *Page 1 Civil War Soldiers - Union - TN - Fold3*, https://www.fold3.com/image/267068122/?xid=1022

Lawless.[40] Note that James Lawless was listed as James
Futrell in the 1870 census. There is no record of Etheldred
ever buying property in Roane County. At some time before
1880, Etheldred's wife Melinda died and, as a widower, he
moved into the household of his son John and his wife
Elizabeth Walls Futrell in District 10 of Morgan County as
indicated in the 1880 census.[41]

Children of Etheldred Futrell and Sarah Martin
were:

    1.1.1   Mary A. Futrell
    1.1.2   John E. Futrell

Children of Etheldred Futrell and Melinda Martin
were:

    1.1.3   Noah Alexander Futrell

Children of Melinda Martin and Jesse Lawless
(stepchildren of Etheldred Futrell) included:

- William Lawless (b. 1838, d. 1 January 1902,
  lived in household of Samuel Martin in 1850)
- Nancy J Lawless (b. 1839)
- Samuel Lawless (b. 1843)

---

[40] Ancestry.com, *1870 United States Federal Census*, Ancestry.com
Operations, Inc:2009, Year: 1870; Census Place: District 16, Roane,
Tennessee; Roll: M593_1555; Page: 519B; Image: 418; Family History
Library Film: 553054
[41] Ancestry.com, *1880 United States Federal Census*, Ancestry.com
Operations, Inc:2010, Year: 1880; Census Place: District 10, Morgan,
Tennessee; Roll: 1273; Family History Film: 1255273; Page: 541D;
Enumeration District: 131

- Pam Lawless (b. 1845)
- James Lawless (b. 4 November 1850, d. 3 November 1933, shown in the household of Melinda Lawless in the 1850 census and in the household of Etheldred and Melinda Futrell in the 1860 census; later was listed as James Futrell in the 1870 Roane County census)

Note: Spelling of the name Lawless in later official records was typically "Lollis"

# Generation 2: Children of Etheldred Futrell

**1.1 Mary A. Futrell**[2] (*Etheldred¹*) was born in Tennessee, presumably in Knox County, around 1843, the first child of Etheldred and Sarah Martin Futrell. She is listed in the household of her parents in the 1850 census in Knox County[42] and in the 1860 census in Roane County.[43] Mary married J.L. Baker in Knox County on 4 November 1862.[44]

Consideration of the time and circumstances leads to interesting speculation about Mary. In 1860, she lived in Roane County, Tennessee, with her father Etheldred, stepmother/aunt Malinda, brother John, half-brother Noah, and cousins/step-siblings Nancy, Pam, and James Lawless. At the time of Mary's marriage in November 1862, both Etheldred and John were in the Union Army in Kentucky, and East Tennessee was largely controlled by Confederate troops. This brings up the question "Where

---

[42] Ancestry.com, *1850 United States Federal Census*, Ancestry.com Operations, Inc:2009, Year: 1850; Census Place: Knoxville, Knox, Tennessee; Roll: M432_886; Page: 107A; Image: 215

[43] Ancestry.com, *1860 United States Federal Census*, Ancestry.com Operations, Inc:2009, Year: 1860; Census Place: District 14, Roane, Tennessee; Roll: M653_1269; Page: 228; Image: 466; Family History Library Film: 805269

[44] Ancestry.com, Tennessee State Marriages, 1780-2002

did J.L. Baker come from and why did the marriage take place in Knox County?"

A review of Roane County census data for 1860 fails to identify a local resident by that name. A review of Knox County census data for 1860 reveals one possibility, a Joseph Baker, son of Morgan and Elizabeth Baker. Is it possible that Joseph knew Mary from her former residency in Knoxville before the Futrells' westward migration to Roane County in the 1850's?

It is also interesting to note that a John Baker served in the 4th Regiment Tennessee Infantry in Cumberland Gap while Etheldred and John Futrell were located there with the 3rd Regiment. John Baker deserted the Union Army on July 8, 1862, just four months before Mary's marriage. Is it possible that John Baker learned of Mary through her father or brother and deserted to go find her?

With Confederates in control of the area, how could J.L. Baker and Mary travel from Roane County to Knox County for their marriage? Is it possible that J.L. Baker was a Confederate soldier stationed in the area?

While these are intriguing possibilities, the fact remains that no official records have been located regarding Mary A. Futrell past her marriage to J.L. Baker, leaving ample opportunity for more advanced research to seek the answers.

**1.2 John E. Futrell[2]** (*Etheldred[1]*)**,** son of Etheldred and Sarah Martin Futrell, was born 1 December 1844 in Tennessee, presumably in Knox County.[45] He is shown in the household of his father, Etheldred Futrell, in Knox County in the 1850 census[46] and in Roane County in the 1860 census.[47]

Along with his father, Etheldred, John Futrell traveled to Flat Lick, Kentucky, where he enlisted in the Union Army on 10 February 1862. John was 17 years old at the time of his enlistment in Company H, 3rd Regiment of the Tennessee Infantry Volunteers. John served out his three-year enlistment in the Union Army.[48] His unit was engaged in major campaigns in Kentucky, Tennessee, and Georgia, including the Atlanta campaign May-September of 1864.[49] John was wounded at the Battle of Murfreesboro, Tennessee in late 1864 where he was shot in the abdomen, resulting in his experiencing an open sore for the

---

[45] Ancestry.com, *Tennessee, Death Records*, 1908-1958, Ancestry.com Operations, Inc:2011, Tennessee State Library and Archives; Nashville, Tennessee; Tennessee Death Records, 1908-1959; Roll #: 69
[46] Ancestry.com, *1850 United States Federal Census*, Ancestry.com Operations, Inc:2009, Year: 1850; Census Place: Knoxville, Knox, Tennessee; Roll: M432_886; Page: 107A; Image: 215
[47] Ancestry.com, *1860 United States Federal Census*, Ancestry.com Operations, Inc:2009, Year: 1860; Census Place: District 14, Roane, Tennessee; Roll: M653_1269; Page: 228; Image: 466; Family History Library Film: 805269
[48] John Futrell Original Discharge Certificate from Union Army
[49] Wikipedia, https://en.wikipedia.org/wiki/3rd_Regiment_Tennessee_Volunteer_Infan try

remainder of his life.[50] John was honorably discharged from the Union Army on 23 February 1865 in Nashville, Tennessee.[51] John's military discharge certificate indicates that he was only four feet eleven inches tall, which supports the family oral tradition that he carried a pack in the Civil War that weighed more than he did.

Eleven months after his military discharge, John married Elizabeth Walls, daughter of John B. and Anna Wolf Walls, on 24 December 1865 in Morgan County, Tennessee.[52] John and Elizabeth were living near her parents and their extended family in District 1 of Morgan County by 1870 as indicated in the 1870 census.[53] This makes John E. Futrell the first member of the Futrell family to become a resident of Morgan County, and other than his father Etheldred, all known Futrell residents of Morgan County since that time have been his descendants. Also living with John and Elizabeth Futrell in 1870 were children Anna (age 3) and Noah (age 1).

---

[50] John Futrell Military Pension Application
[51] John Futrell Original Discharge Certificate from Union Army
[52] Ancestry.com, Tennessee State Marriages, 1780-2002
[53] Ancestry.com, *1870 United States Federal Census*, Ancestry.com Operations, Inc:2009, Year: 1870; Census Place: District 1, Morgan, Tennessee; Roll: M593_1552; Page: 2A; Image: 8; Family History Library Film: 553051

*Figure 3. John Futrell and Elizabeth Walls Futrell*

    1.3.6   John Albert Futrell
    1.3.7   George W. Futrell

All available U.S. censuses list John's occupation as farm worker or farmer. However, his death certificate indicates that he was a shoe cobbler, just like his father Etheldred and his half-brother Noah.[54]

John's first wife, Elizabeth, died in 1913.[55] He then married Nellie Byrd on 29 September 1914 in Morgan County.[56] Nellie had previously been married to John

---

[54] Ancestry.com, *Tennessee, Death Records, 1908-1958*, Ancestry.com Operations, Inc:2011
[55] Ancestry.com, *U.S., Find A Grave Index, 1600s-Current*, Ancestry.com Operations, Inc:2012
[56] Ancestry.com, Tennessee State Marriages, 1780-2002

Macy[57] and William A. Walls.[58] John Futrell died on 23
November 1917[59] and was buried beside Elizabeth in the
Coalhill Cemetery in Morgan County.

[57] Jordan R. Dodd, *Tennessee, Marriages, 1851-1900*, Ancestry.com
Operations, Inc:2000
[58] Ancestry.com, Tennessee State Marriages, 1780-2002
[59] Ancestry.com, *Tennessee, Death Records, 1908-1958*

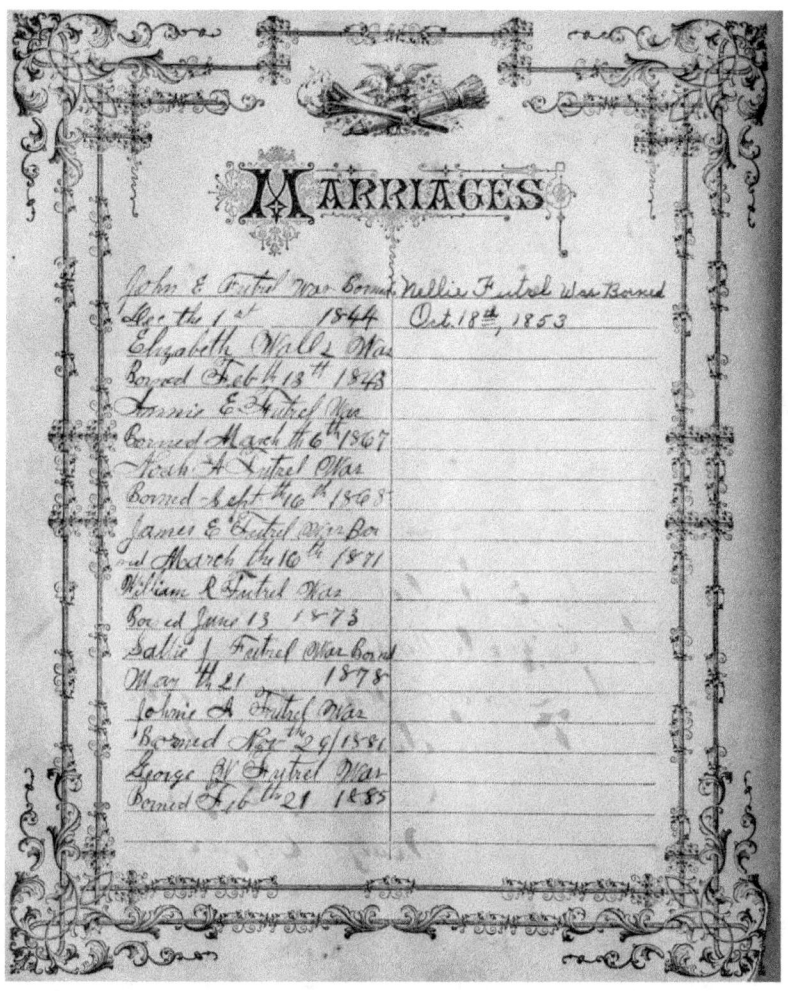

*Figure 4. Page from John Futrell's family Bible indicating family names and dates of birth. Note that the page for family marriages was incorrectly used to record birth dates.*

**1.3 Noah Alexander Futrell**[2] (*Etheldred¹*) was born 16 March 1852 in Knox County, Tennessee, the son of Etheldred and Melinda Martin Futrell. He is shown in the household of his father, Etheldred Futrell, in Roane County in the 1860 census.[60]

Noah married Sarafina Edwards on 25 April 1869 in Roane County.[61] He is listed in the 1870 census as head of household in District 16 of Roane County, living with his wife and 6-month old son. His occupation is listed as Farm Laborer.[62] Sarafina died in December 1879 of consumption,[63] leaving Noah to raise three young children. In 1900, Noah lived with his son Etheldred T. Futrell in District 14 of Roane County.[64] By 1910, Noah lived alone in District 2 of Roane County, and was listed as a shoemaker

---

[60] Ancestry.com, *1860 United States Federal Census*, Ancestry.com Operations, Inc:2009, Year: 1860; Census Place: District 14, Roane, Tennessee; Roll: M653_1269; Page: 228; Image: 466; Family History Library Film: 805269

[61] Ancestry.com, Tennessee State Marriages, 1780-2002

[62] Ancestry.com, *1870 United States Federal Census*, Ancestry.com Operations, Inc:2009, Year: 1870; Census Place: District 16, Roane, Tennessee; Roll: M593_1555; Page: 520A; Image: 419; Family History Library Film: 553054

[63] Ancestry.com, *U.S. Federal Census Mortality Schedules, 1850-1885*, Ancestry.com Operations, Inc:2010; National Archives and Records Administration (NARA); Washington, D.C.; Federal Mortality Census Schedules, 1850-1880, and Related Indexes, 1850-1880; Archive Collection: T655; Archive Roll Number: 30; Census Year: 1879; Census Place: District 5 and 14, Roane, Tennessee

[64] Ancestry.com, *1900 United States Federal Census*, Ancestry.com Operations, Inc:2004, Year: 1900; Census Place: Civil District 14, Roane, Tennessee; Roll: 1593; Page: 19B; Enumeration District: 0116; FHL microfilm: 1241593

owning his own shop.[65] Noah continued to live alone in District 2 of Roane County in the 1920 census with general farming listed as his occupation.[66] Records show that Noah Futrell joined Little Emory Primitive Baptist Church in 1906[67] and he and his son Etheldred were trustees when the church building was sold to Big Emory Missionary Baptist Church on 23 April 1928.[68] Noah died 22 July 1928 and is buried in the Edwards Cemetery in Roane County.[69]

Children of Noah and Sarafina Edwards Futrell included:

    1.3.1   Etheldred T. Futrell
    1.3.2   Malinda Ann Futrell
    1.3.3   Elizabeth "Betty" Jane Futrell

---

[65] Ancestry.com, *1910 United States Federal Census*, Ancestry.com Operations, Inc:2006, Year: 1910; Census Place: Oliver Springs, Roane, Tennessee; Roll: T624_1517; Page: 2A; Enumeration District: 0150; FHL microfilm: 1375530

[66] Ancestry.com, *1920 United States Federal Census*, Ancestry.com Operations, Inc:2010, Year: 1920; Census Place: Civil District 2, Roane, Tennessee; Roll: T625_1760; Page: 7B; Enumeration District: 161; Image: 817

[67] Minutes of the One Hundred and Sixth Annual Session of the Hiwassee Association of Primitive Baptists, L.L. Thomas, Clerk:1928

[68] Roane County Heritage Book Committee and County Heritage, Inc., *The Heritage of Roane County, Tennessee 1801-1999*, Kingston, Tennessee:1999

[69] Ancestry.com, *Tennessee, Death Records*, 1908-1958, Ancestry.com Operations, Inc:2011, Tennessee State Library and Archives; Nashville, Tennessee; Tennessee Death Records, 1908-1959; Roll #: 7

# Generations 3 and 4: Descendants of John E. Futrell

## Anna Elizabeth Futrell Overton Family

**1.2.1 Anna Elizabeth Futrell**[3] (*John E.*[2], *Etheldred*[1]), daughter of John E. and Elizabeth Walls Futrell, was born 6 March 1867 in Morgan County, Tennessee.[70] She married William John "Bill" Overton on 26 September 1897 in Morgan County.[71] Bill was previously married to Josephine Patterson, who reportedly died in 1897, three months after their marriage. Anna and Bill lived on a farm in East Roane County where they are found in District 18 in the 1900 census.[72] Anna reportedly died during childbirth[73] in 1907 and was buried in the Coalhill Cemetery in Morgan County.[74] Bill died two years later on 26 February 1909[75] and is buried in the Lawnville Cemetery in Roane County.[76]

---

[70] John E. Futrell Family Bible record

[71] Ancestry.com, Tennessee State Marriages, 1780-2002

[72] Ancestry.com, *1900 United States Federal Census*, Ancestry.com Operations, Inc:2004, Year: 1900; Census Place: Civil District 18, Roane, Tennessee; Roll: 1593; Page: 12A; Enumeration District: 0114; FHL microfilm: 1241593

[73] Per family member Shirley Overton Smith

[74] Ancestry.com, *U.S., Find A Grave Index, 1600s-Current*, Ancestry.com Operations, Inc:2012

[75] Ancestry.com, *Tennessee, Death Records, 1908-1958*, Ancestry.com Operations, Inc:2011

[76] Ancestry.com, *U.S., Find A Grave Index, 1600s-Current*, Ancestry.com Operations, Inc:2012

After the death of both parents, the couples' four young children lived with their grandparents, Robert W. and Lucie Overton, in Civil District 3 of Roane County, as shown in the 1910 census.[77]

Note: Bill's middle name is sometimes shown as "Jesse" rather than "John"; however, the death certificate of his son John indicates that his name was John William Overton, Sr.

**1.2.1.1 Lucy Elizabeth Overton**[4] (*Anna Futrell[3], John E.[2], Etheldred[1]*), daughter of William John and Anna Elizabeth Futrell Overton, was born 17 August 1898 in Tennessee[78], presumably in Roane County. She married George Thomas Poland on 15 February 1918 in Roane County[79]. Lucy died on 10 December 1934 in Harriman, Roane County[80]. George died on 11 October 1953 in Harriman[81]. Both are buried in the Piney Grove Cemetery in Midtown, Roane County[82].

---

[77] Ancestry.com, *1910 United States Federal Census*, Ancestry.com Operations, Inc:2006, Year: 1910; Year: 1910; Census Place: Civil District 3, Roane, Tennessee; Roll: T624_1517; Page: 2A; Enumeration District: 0153; FHL microfilm: 1375530

[78] Ancestry.com, *Tennessee, Death Records*, 1908-1958, Ancestry.com Operations, Inc:2011

[79] Ancestry.com, Tennessee State Marriages, 1780-2002

[80] Ancestry.com, *Tennessee, Death Records*, 1908-1958, Ancestry.com Operations, Inc:2011, Tennessee State Library and Archives; Nashville, Tennessee; Tennessee Death Records, 1908-1959; Roll #: 12

[81] Ancestry.com, *Tennessee, Death Records*, 1908-1958, Ancestry.com Operations, Inc:2011

[82] Ancestry.com, *U.S., Find A Grave Index, 1600s-Current*, Ancestry.com Operations, Inc:2012

**1.2.1.2 Margaret Robbie Overton**[4] (*Anna Futrell*[3], *John E.*[2], *Etheldred*[1]), daughter of William John and Anna Elizabeth Futrell Overton, was born 2 November 1899 in Lawnville, Roane County, Tennessee[83]. She married James Harvey Harmon on 7 November 1924 in Roane County[84]. The 1930 census shows James and Robbie living on Clinch Street in Harriman, Roane County[85]. They remained local residents until their death. James died on 5 May 1956 in Harriman[86] and Robbie died on 13 April 1991, also in Harriman[87]. Both are buried in the Harriman Cemetery in the Walnut Hill section of Harriman[88].

**1.2.1.3 John William Overton, Jr.**[4] (*Anna Futrell*[3], *John E.*[2], *Etheldred*[1]), son of William John and Anna Elizabeth Futrell Overton, was born 26 April 1901 in Tennessee[89], presumably in Roane County. After serving in the military, John married Loula Bertha Cassada, originally from Pulaski County, Kentucky,[90] in Morgan

---

[83] Ancestry.com, *U.S., Find A Grave Index, 1600s-Current*, Ancestry.com Operations, Inc:2012

[84] Ancestry.com, Tennessee State Marriages, 1780-2002

[85] Ancestry.com, *U.S., Find A Grave Index, 1600s-Current*, Ancestry.com Operations, Inc:2012

[86] Ancestry.com, *U.S., Find A Grave Index, 1600s-Current*, Ancestry.com Operations, Inc:2012

[87] Ancestry.com, *U.S., Find A Grave Index, 1600s-Current*, Ancestry.com Operations, Inc:2012

[88] Ancestry.com, *U.S., Find A Grave Index, 1600s-Current*, Ancestry.com Operations, Inc:2012

[89] From family Bible record per family member Shirley Overton Smith

[90] Ancestry.com, *1900 United States Federal Census*, Ancestry.com Operations, Inc:2004, Year: 1900; Census Place: Sloans Valley, Pulaski,

County, Tennessee on 12 November 1922[91]. John then married Willie Frank Wilson in Carter County, Tennessee on 14 June 1924 using the name "John N. Overson"[92]. John was admitted to the National Home for Disabled Volunteer Soldiers in Johnson City, Tennessee on 1 July 1924, and was readmitted to the veteran's home four times during the next nine years[93]. Bertha died on 1 January 1929 in Harriman, Roane County, Tennessee[94]. John married Louise Dixon in Carter County on 16 March 1929[95]. John's later marriage to Jewell Elizabeth Richards in Bristol, Virginia on 1 January 1940 is confirmed by the listing of each of his parents on the license[96]. John died in Johnson City, Washington County, Tennessee on 10 February 1954 and is buried in the Andrew Johnson National Cemetery in Greeneville, Tennessee[97]. Note that some records list his name as William J. while others list it as John William.

Kentucky; Roll: 549; Page: 6A; Enumeration District: 0120; FHL microfilm: 1240549

[91] Ancestry.com, Tennessee State Marriages, 1780-2002

[92] Ancestry.com, Tennessee State Marriages, 1780-2002

[93] Ancestry.com, U.S. National Homes for Disabled Volunteer Soldiers, 1866-1938, Ancestry.com Operations, Inc:2007

[94] Ancestry.com, *Tennessee, Death Records*, 1908-1958, Ancestry.com Operations, Inc:2011, Tennessee State Library and Archives; Nashville, Tennessee; Tennessee Death Records, 1908-1959; Roll #: 2

[95] Ancestry.com, Tennessee State Marriages, 1780-2002

[96] Ancestry.com, *Virginia, Marriage Records, 1936-2014*, Ancestry.com Operations, Inc:2015

[97] Ancestry.com, U.S. National Cemetery Interment Control Forms, 1928-1962, Ancestry.com Operations, Inc:2012

**1.2.1.4 Joseph Dedrick "Joe" Overton**[4] (*Anna Futrell*[3], *John E.*[2], *Etheldred*[1]), son of William John and Anna Elizabeth Futrell Overton, was born 22 October 1904 in Tennessee[98], presumably in Roane County. He married Fannie Elizabeth Jones on 30 July 1927 in Roane County[99]. Joe died 17 December 1980 in Harriman, Roane County[100]. Fannie died on 15 March 1999 while living in Kingston, Roane County[101]. Both are buried in Roane Memorial Gardens, Roane County[102].

## Noah A. Futrell Family

**1.2.2 Noah A. Futrell**[3] (*John E.*[2], *Etheldred*[1]), son of John E. and Elizabeth Walls Futrell, was born 16 September 1868 in Morgan County, Tennessee.[103] About 1898, he married Mary Jane Cheek, who had previously been married to C.K. Robbins[104] and Robert A. Walls.[105] Noah and Mary Jane moved to Lucas County, Ohio before

---

[98] Ancestry.com, *U.S., Social Security Death Index, 1935-2014*, Ancestry.com Operations, Inc:2011, Number: 414-20-9686; Issue State: Tennessee; Issue Date: Before 1951

[99] Ancestry.com, Tennessee State Marriages, 1780-2002

[100] Ancestry.com, *U.S., Social Security Death Index, 1935-2014*, Ancestry.com Operations, Inc:2011, Number: 414-20-9686; Issue State: Tennessee; Issue Date: Before 1951

[101] Ancestry.com, *U.S., Social Security Death Index, 1935-2014*, Ancestry.com Operations, Inc:2011, Number: 413-94-3274; Issue State: Tennessee; Issue Date: 1969

[102] Per family member Shirley Overton Smith

[103] John E. Futrell Family Bible record

[104] Ancestry.com, Tennessee State Marriages, 1780-2002

[105] Ancestry.com, Tennessee State Marriages, 1780-2002

1920.[106] Mary died on 31 January 1929 in Lucas County[107] and Noah died a few months later in Lucas County on 17 December 1929.[108]

**1.2.2.1 John L. Futrell**[4] *(Noah A.[3], John E.[2], Etheldred[1])*, son of Noah A. and Mary Jane Cheek Futrell, was born 7 June 1899 in Coalfield, Morgan County, Tennessee.[109] He moved to Toledo, Lucas County, Ohio before 1920[110] and married Margaret Mamie LNU. Mamie died in Toledo on 14 May 1974[111] and John died on 11 October 1981.[112]

**1.2.2.2 Speedy Albert Futrell**[4] *(Noah A.[3], John E.[2], Etheldred[1])*, son of Noah A. and Mary Jane Cheek Futrell, was born 7 July 1906 in Coalfield, Morgan County, Tennessee.[113] Speedy moved to Toledo, Lucas County, Ohio

---

[106] Ancestry.com, *1920 United States Federal Census*, Ancestry.com Operations, Inc:2010, Year: 1920; Census Place: Toledo Ward 3, Lucas, Ohio; Roll: T625_1407; Page: 5B; Enumeration District: 42; Image: 789

[107] Ancestry.com and Ohio Department of Health, *Ohio, Deaths, 1908-1932, 1938-2007*, Ancestry.com Operations, Inc:2010

[108] Ancestry.com and Ohio Department of Health, *Ohio, Deaths, 1908-1932, 1938-2007*, Ancestry.com Operations, Inc:2010

[109] Ancestry.com, *Tennessee, Delayed Birth Records, 1869-1909*, Ancestry.com Operations, Inc:2012

[110] Ancestry.com, *1920 United States Federal Census*, Ancestry.com Operations, Inc:2010, Year: 1920; Census Place: Toledo Ward 14, Lucas, Ohio; Roll: T625_1411; Page: 7B; Enumeration District: 149; Image: 764

[111] Ancestry.com and Ohio Department of Health, *Ohio, Deaths, 1908-1932, 1938-2007*, Ancestry.com Operations, Inc:2010

[112] Ancestry.com and Ohio Department of Health, *Ohio, Deaths, 1908-1932, 1938-2007*, Ancestry.com Operations, Inc:2010

[113] Ancestry.com, *Tennessee, Delayed Birth Records, 1869-1909*, Ancestry.com Operations, Inc:2012

with his parents before 1920.[114] He married before 1940, but in the 1940 census, he was living with his half-sister Emily and her husband in Toledo.[115] His wife was not present in the household in 1940. Speedy later moved to North Carolina, where his wife Edna S. LNU died in Waynesville, Haywood County in 1977.[116] Speedy died in Asheville, Buncombe County on 28 September 1985.[117] Both Speedy and Edna are buried in Garrett-Hillcrest Memorial Park in Waynesville, North Carolina.[118]

### Stepchildren of Noah A. Futrell

Children of Mary Jane Cheek and C.K. Robbins

- Hester Robbins
- James Robbins
- Rosa Robbins

Children of Mary Jane Cheek and Robert A. Walls

- Emily Walls

---

[114] Ancestry.com, *1920 United States Federal Census*, Ancestry.com Operations, Inc:2010, Year: 1920; Census Place: Toledo Ward 14, Lucas, Ohio; Roll: T625_1411; Page: 7B; Enumeration District: 149; Image: 764

[115] Ancestry.com, *1940 United States Federal Census*, Ancestry.com Operations, Inc:2010, Year: 1940; Year: 1940; Census Place: Toledo, Lucas, Ohio; Roll: T627_3258; Page: 11A; Enumeration District: 95-44

[116] Ancestry.com, *U.S., Find A Grave Index, 1600s-Current*, Ancestry.com Operations, Inc:2012

[117] Ancestry.com, *U.S., Social Security Death Index, 1935-2014*, Ancestry.com Operations, Inc:2011, Number: 299-05-5168; Issue State: Ohio; Issue Date: Before 1951

[118] Ancestry.com, Web: North Carolina, Find A Grave Index, 1716-2012, Ancestry.com Operations, Inc:2012

# James Etheldred Futrell Family

**1.2.3 James Etheldred Futrell[3]** (*John E.[2], Etheldred[1]*), son of John E. and Elizabeth Walls Futrell, was born 16 March 1871 in Morgan County, Tennessee.[119] He married Mahala Luiza Adcock, daughter of Archibald and Martha Jackson Adcock on 7 May 1891.[120] James and Mahala had two sons. Mahala died on 14 September 1910 and was buried in the Adcock Cemetery in Coalfield.[121] James then married Sarah A. "Sally" Farr on 6 March 1911 in Morgan County.[122] James and Sally had three daughters. James died on 30 October 1934 and was buried in the Adcock cemetery in Coalfield.[123]

## Children of James Etheldred and Mahala Luiza Adcock Futrell:

**1.2.3.1 Albert Harrison Futrell[4]** (*James[3], John E.[2], Etheldred[1]*), son of James Etheldred and Mahala Luiza Adcock Futrell, was born in Coalfield, Morgan County on 21 June 1892.[124] He married Lelah A. Hill on 21 November

---

[119] John E. Futrell Family Bible record

[120] Ancestry.com, Tennessee State Marriages, 1780-2002

[121] Ancestry.com, *Tennessee, Death Records*, 1908-1958, Ancestry.com Operations, Inc:2011, Tennessee State Library and Archives; Nashville, Tennessee; Tennessee Death Records, 1908-1959; Roll #: 23

[122] Ancestry.com, Tennessee State Marriages, 1780-2002

[123] Ancestry.com, *Tennessee, Death Records*, 1908-1958, Ancestry.com Operations, Inc:2011, Tennessee State Library and Archives; Nashville, Tennessee; Tennessee Death Records, 1908-1959; Roll #: 12

[124] Ancestry.com, *Tennessee, Delayed Birth Records, 1869-1909*, Ancestry.com Operations, Inc:2012

1914 in Morgan County.[125] Albert and Lelah lived on Coalhill Road near the intersection of Authorn Sheldon Road. Lelah died on 14 November 1959[126] and Albert died on 14 April 1965.[127] Both are buried in the Adcock Cemetery in Coalfield.

**1.2.3.2 William Homer Futrell**[4] (*James³, John E.², Etheldred¹*), son of James Etheldred and Mahala Luiza Adcock Futrell, was born in Coalfield, Morgan County, Tennessee on 26 December 1900.[128] Homer is shown living in Lorain, Ohio working at a steel mill in the 1920 census.[129] He married Beulah Mae Woods on 25 January 1922 in Morgan County.[130] Homer and Beulah returned to Lorain, Ohio where they are found in the 1940 census.[131]

---

[125] Ancestry.com, Tennessee State Marriages, 1780-2002
[126] Ancestry.com, *U.S., Find A Grave Index, 1600s-Current*, Ancestry.com Operations, Inc:2012
[127] Ancestry.com, *U.S., Find A Grave Index, 1600s-Current*, Ancestry.com Operations, Inc:2012
[128] Ancestry.com, *Tennessee, Delayed Birth Records, 1869-1909*, Ancestry.com Operations, Inc:2012
[129] Ancestry.com, *1940 United States Federal Census*, Ancestry.com Operations, Inc:2010, Year: 1940; Year: 1940; Census Place: Lorain Ward 3, Lorain, Ohio; Roll: T625_1406; Page: 18B; Enumeration District: 14; Image: 67
[130] Ancestry.com, Tennessee State Marriages, 1780-2002
[131] Ancestry.com, *1940 United States Federal Census*, Ancestry.com Operations, Inc:2010, Year: 1940; Year: 1940; Census Place: Lorain, Lorain, Ohio; Roll: T627_3102; Page: 10A; Enumeration District: 47-24

Homer died in Mount Vernon, Ohio on 2 May 1957.[132]

Beulah died in Lorain, Ohio on 24 May 1973.[133]

**Children of James Etheldred and Sally Farr Futrell**

**1.2.3.3 Martha Futrell**[4] (*James³, John E.²,
Etheldred¹*), daughter of James Etheldred and Sally Farr
Futrell, was born 15 July 1914 in Morgan County,
Tennessee.[134] She married John Burton Humphreys on 4
March 1933 in Morgan County.[135] Martha and Burton lived
in Coalfield in 1940 with their daughter Christine.[136]
Burton died in July 1986 in Harriman, Roane County.[137]
Martha died on 2 October 2005 in Harriman.[138]

**1.2.3.4 Vesta Futrell**[4] (*James³, John E.²,
Etheldred¹*), daughter of James Etheldred and Sally Farr
Futrell, was born 20 September 1916, most likely in

---

[132] Ancestry.com and Ohio Department of Health, **Ohio, Deaths, 1908-1932, 1938-2007**, Ancestry.com Operations, Inc:2010
[133] Ancestry.com and Ohio Department of Health, **Ohio, Deaths, 1908-1932, 1938-2007**, Ancestry.com Operations, Inc:2010
[134] Ancestry.com, *U.S., Social Security Death Index, 1935-2014*, Ancestry.com Operations, Inc:2011, Issue State: Tennessee; Issue Date: Before 1951
[135] Ancestry.com, Tennessee State Marriages, 1780-2002
[136] Ancestry.com, *1940 United States Federal Census*, Ancestry.com Operations, Inc:2010, Year: 1940; Year: 1940; Census Place: Morgan, Tennessee; Roll: T627_3924; Page: 20B; Enumeration District: 65-1
[137] Ancestry.com, *U.S., Social Security Death Index, 1935-2014*, Ancestry.com Operations, Inc:2011, Number: 414-16-4445; Issue State: Tennessee; Issue Date: Before 1951
[138] Ancestry.com, *U.S., Social Security Death Index, 1935-2014*, Ancestry.com Operations, Inc:2011, Issue State: Tennessee; Issue Date: Before 1951

Coalfield, Morgan County, Tennessee.[139] She married Ferry Arnold Shipwash on 3 July 1934 in Roane County, Tennessee.[140] They lived in Harriman, Roane County before moving to Lorain, Ohio by 1945.[141] Arnold died in Lorain on 12 August 1984.[142] Vesta died 25 November 2009 in Amherst Township, Ohio and is buried in Ridge Hill Memorial Park.[143]

**1.2.3.5 Mary Alice Futrell**[4] (*James*[3], *John E.*[2], *Etheldred*[1]), daughter of James Etheldred and Sally Farr Futrell, was born 15 July 1924, most likely in Coalfield, Morgan County, Tennessee.[144] She married Eblen Major Liles on 15 April 1940 in Morgan County.[145] Eblen died on 19 February 1991.[146] Mary Alice moved to Anderson County, Tennessee after her husband's death where she

---

[139] Ancestry.com, *U.S., Social Security Death Index, 1935-2014*, Ancestry.com Operations, Inc:2011, Issue State: Tennessee; Issue Date: Before 1951

[140] Ancestry.com, Tennessee State Marriages, 1780-2002

[141] Ancestry.com, *1940 United States Federal Census*, Ancestry.com Operations, Inc:2010, Year: 1940; Year: 1940; Census Place: Harriman, Roane, Tennessee; Roll: T627_3929; Page: 7B; Enumeration District: 73-2

[142] Ancestry.com, *U.S., Social Security Death Index, 1935-2014*, Ancestry.com Operations, Inc:2011, Number: 408-03-2772; Issue State: Tennessee; Issue Date: Before 1951

[143] Ancestry.com, *U.S., Social Security Death Index, 1935-2014*, Ancestry.com Operations, Inc:2011; Issue State: Tennessee; Issue Date: Before 1951

[144] Gravestone inscription, Coalhill Cemetery, Coalhill, Morgan County, Tennessee

[145] Ancestry.com, Tennessee State Marriages, 1780-2002

[146] Ancestry.com, *U.S., Social Security Death Index, 1935-2014*, Ancestry.com Operations, Inc:2011, Number: 410-07-4067; Issue State: Tennessee; Issue Date: Before 1951

died on 2 April 2016. Both are buried in the Coalhill
Cemetery in Morgan County.

> *Mary Alice Futrell Liles was the last known survivor of
> the first four generations of the Futrell family of East
> Tennessee.*

## William Robert Futrell Family

**1.2.4 William Robert "Bob" Futrell**[3] (*John E.*[2],
*Etheldred*[1]), son of John E. and Elizabeth Walls Futrell,
was born 13 June 1873, presumably in Morgan County,
Tennessee.[147] He married Margaret "Maggie" Leona Fry,
daughter of Melvin Fry and Permelia Catherine Hughes on
5 May 1895 in Morgan County.[148] They established a
household in the Coalhill Community near Coalfield in
Morgan County where he worked as a farmer. Bob was an
invalid most of his life after 1900 and was generally
bedfast. Maggie died in Coalfield on 5 August 1935 and
was buried in the Ritter Cemetery in the Coalhill
Community of Morgan County.[149] Bob died in Harriman,
Roane County, on 29 March 1939 and was also buried in
the Ritter Cemetery.[150]

---

[147] John E. Futrell Family Bible record
[148] Ancestry.com, Tennessee State Marriages, 1780-2002
[149] Ancestry.com, *Tennessee, Death Records*, 1908-1958, Ancestry.com
Operations, Inc:2011, Tennessee State Library and Archives; Nashville,
Tennessee; Tennessee Death Records, 1908-1959; Roll #: 9
[150] Ancestry.com, *Tennessee, Death Records*, 1908-1958, Ancestry.com
Operations, Inc:2011, Tennessee State Library and Archives; Nashville,
Tennessee; Tennessee Death Records, 1908-1959; Roll #: 3

*Figure 5. William Robert and Margaret Leona Fry Futrell Family. L-R Lonnie (seated), Clarence, Conard, Bob (seated), Lewis (standing in front), Carrie, Maggie (seated), Georgia Evamay (in Maggie's lap), and Ella. Photo taken about 1914.*

**1.2.4.1 Leonard Futrell**[4] (*William*[3], *John E.*[2], *Etheldred*[1]), son of William Robert and Margaret Leona Fry Futrell, was born in 1896, presumably in Morgan County, Tennessee and died in infancy the same year. He is buried in the Ritter Cemetery, Morgan County.[151]

**1.2.4.2 Lonnie Earnest Futrell**[4] (*William*[3], *John E.*[2], *Etheldred*[1]), son of William Robert and Margaret Leona Fry Futrell, was born 15 June 1897 in Morgan County, Tennessee.[152] He married Ira Jackson 9 January 1921 in Morgan County.[153] Lonnie established a home on

---

[151] Gravestone inscription, Ritter Cemetery, Coalhill, Morgan County, Tennessee

[152] Ancestry.com, *U.S., World War I Draft Registration Cards, 1917-1918*, Ancestry.com Operations, Inc:2005, Registration State: Tennessee; Registration County: Morgan; Roll: 1877598

[153] Ancestry.com, Tennessee State Marriages, 1780-2002

Vic Justice Road in Back Valley near Coalfield in Morgan
County and moved to Roane County late in life. Lonnie
initially worked as a coal miner and later retired from
Yankee Lumber Company in Harriman. He died 14 March
1982[154] and Ira died on 9 May 1993.[155] Both are buried in
the Estes Cemetery in Coalfield.[156]

**1.2.4.3 Clarence Maynard Futrell**[4] (*William[3],
John E.[2], Etheldred[1]*), son of William Robert and Margaret
Leona Fry Futrell, was born 18 May 1900 in Morgan
County, Tennessee.[157] Clarence married Sadie Frances
Thornton on 19 September 1923.[158] They lived on
Cumberland Road in Coalfield until Clarence's death on 22
August 1971.[159] Clarence worked as a coal miner
throughout his life. Frances died on 1 October 1978 in

---

[154] Ancestry.com, *U.S., Social Security Death Index, 1935-2014*,
Ancestry.com Operations, Inc:2011, Number: 408-01-2739; Issue State:
Tennessee; Issue Date: Before 1951
[155] Ancestry.com, *U.S., Find A Grave Index, 1600s-Current*,
Ancestry.com Operations, Inc:2012
[156] Ancestry.com, *U.S., Find A Grave Index, 1600s-Current*,
Ancestry.com Operations, Inc:2012
[157] Ancestry.com, *U.S., Social Security Death Index, 1935-2014*,
Ancestry.com Operations, Inc:2011, Number: 409-05-9031; Issue State:
Tennessee; Issue Date: Before 1951
[158] Ancestry.com, Tennessee State Marriages, 1780-2002
[159] Ancestry.com, *U.S., Social Security Death Index, 1935-2014*,
Ancestry.com Operations, Inc:2011, Number: 409-05-9031; Issue State:
Tennessee; Issue Date: Before 1951

Clinton, Tennessee.[160] Both are buried in the Thornton Cemetery in Back Valley in Morgan County.[161]

### 1.2.4.4 James Conrad "Conard" Futrell[4]

(*William[3], John E.[2], Etheldred[1]*), son of William Robert and Margaret Leona Fry Futrell, was born 11 September 1903 in Morgan County, Tennessee.[162] Conard married Sadie Morrison 21 July 1927 in Roane County.[163] They lived on Fairview Road adjacent to the Pleasant Grove Baptist Church in Coalfield, Morgan County. Conard died on 25 September 1979[164] and Sadie died on 15 October 2001.[165] Both Conard and Sadie are buried in the Estes Cemetery in Coalfield.[166]

### 1.2.4.5 Ella Mae "Eller" Futrell[4] (*William[3], John E.[2], Etheldred[1]*), daughter of William Robert and Margaret Leona Fry Futrell, was born 30 April 1906 in Morgan

---

[160] Ancestry.com, *U.S., Find A Grave Index, 1600s-Current*, Ancestry.com Operations, Inc:2012

[161] Ancestry.com, *U.S., Find A Grave Index, 1600s-Current*, Ancestry.com Operations, Inc:2012

[162] Ancestry.com, *Tennessee, Delayed Birth Records, 1869-1909*, Ancestry.com Operations, Inc:2012

[163] Ancestry.com, Tennessee State Marriages, 1780-2002

[164] Ancestry.com, *U.S., Social Security Death Index, 1935-2014*, Ancestry.com Operations, Inc:2011, Number: 409-05-1983; Issue State: Tennessee; Issue Date: Before 1951

[165] Ancestry.com, *U.S., Social Security Death Index, 1935-2014*, Ancestry.com Operations, Inc:2011, Number: 411-08-4725; Issue State: Tennessee; Issue Date: Before 1951

[166] Ancestry.com, *U.S., Find A Grave Index, 1600s-Current*, Ancestry.com Operations, Inc:2012

County, Tennessee.[167] She married Henry Elmer Clark on 22 January 1925 in Roane County.[168] After initially living in Coalfield, they moved to Roane County after 1940.[169] Henry died on 30 April 1983[170] and Eller died six years later on 2 January 1989.[171] Both are buried in Roane Memorial Gardens in Roane County.[172]

**1.2.4.6 Carrie Luvena Futrell**[4] (*William³, John E.², Etheldred¹*), daughter of William Robert and Margaret Leona Fry Futrell, was born on 13 March 1908 in Morgan County, Tennessee.[173] She married Paul Aleck Humphreys 7 August 1927 in Roane County.[174] They initially lived in Coalfield, but moved to Roane County between 1935 and

---

[167] Ancestry.com, *U.S., Social Security Death Index, 1935-2014*, Ancestry.com Operations, Inc:2011, Number: 408-44-7905; Issue State: Tennessee; Issue Date: Before 1951

[168] Ancestry.com, Tennessee State Marriages, 1780-2002

[169] Ancestry.com, *1940 United States Federal Census*, Ancestry.com Operations, Inc:2010, Year: 1940; Year: 1940; Census Place: Morgan, Tennessee; Roll: T627_3924; Page: 2B; Enumeration District: 65-1

[170] Ancestry.com, *U.S., Social Security Death Index, 1935-2014*, Ancestry.com Operations, Inc:2011, Number: 415-03-6846; Issue State: Tennessee; Issue Date: Before 1951

[171] Ancestry.com, *U.S., Social Security Death Index, 1935-2014*, Ancestry.com Operations, Inc:2011, Number: 408-44-7905; Issue State: Tennessee; Issue Date: Before 1951

[172] Ancestry.com, *U.S., Find A Grave Index, 1600s-Current*, Ancestry.com Operations, Inc:2012

[173] Gravestone inscription, Sugar Grove Cemetery, Roane County, Tennessee

[174] Ancestry.com, Tennessee State Marriages, 1780-2002

1940.[175] Paul died on 26 September 1956.[176] Carrie continued to live in Roane County until her death on 7 May 2004.[177] Both are buried in Sugar Grove Baptist Church Cemetery in Roane County.[178]

**1.2.4.7 Lewis Lawrence Futrell**[4] (*William³, John E.², Etheldred¹*), son of William Robert and Margaret Leona Fry Futrell, was born 18 December 1910 in Morgan County.[179] He married Lassie Phoebe King on 3 July 1932 in Anderson County.[180] They initially lived in the Coalfield Camp, then bought property on Lower Jackson Road in the late 1930s where they lived until their deaths. Lewis initially worked as a coal miner from the age of ten, then worked as a maintenance mechanic at the Oak Ridge K-25 Plant, and finally retired from his job as a corrections officer with the State of Tennessee. Lewis was an ordained Baptist minister and pastored several churches in the Coalfield area during later life. Lewis died on 23 June

---

[175] Ancestry.com, *1940 United States Federal Census*, Ancestry.com Operations, Inc:2010, Year: 1940; Census Place: Harriman, Roane, Tennessee; Roll: T627_3929; Page: 2A; Enumeration District: 73-1

[176] Ancestry.com, *Tennessee, Death Records*, 1908-1958, Ancestry.com Operations, Inc:2011, Tennessee State Library and Archives; Nashville, Tennessee; Tennessee Death Records, 1908-1959

[177] Gravestone inscription, Sugar Grove Cemetery, Roane County, Tennessee

[178] Gravestone inscription, Sugar Grove Cemetery, Roane County, Tennessee

[179] Ancestry.com, *U.S., Social Security Death Index, 1935-2014*, Ancestry.com Operations, Inc:2011, Number: 409-03-0067; Issue State: Tennessee; Issue Date: Before 1951

[180] Ancestry.com, Tennessee State Marriages, 1780-2002

1995[181] in Roane County and Lassie died on 5 July 2000 in Anderson County.[182] Both are buried in Roane Memorial Gardens in Roane County.[183]

**1.2.4.8 Georgia Evamay Futrell**[4] (*William*[3]*, John E.*[2]*, Etheldred*[1]), daughter of William Robert and Margaret Leona Fry Futrell, was born 1 October 1913 in Morgan County, Tennessee.[184] The entire family, except for Margaret Leona, contracted the flu during the pandemic of 1918. Georgia died at home in Morgan County two weeks past her fifth birthday on 15 October 1918 from the flu.[185] She is buried in the Ritter Cemetery in the Coalhill Community of Morgan County.[186]

---

[181] Ancestry.com, *U.S., Social Security Death Index, 1935-2014*, Ancestry.com Operations, Inc:2011, Number: 409-03-0067; Issue State: Tennessee; Issue Date: Before 1951

[182] Ancestry.com, *U.S., Social Security Death Index, 1935-2014*, Ancestry.com Operations, Inc:2011, Number: 412-17-3465; Issue State: Tennessee; Issue Date: 1974

[183] Gravestone inscription, Roane Memorial Gardens, Roane County, Tennessee

[184] Ancestry.com, *Tennessee, Death Records*, 1908-1958, Ancestry.com Operations, Inc:2011, Tennessee State Library and Archives; Nashville, Tennessee; Tennessee Death Records, 1908-1959; Roll #:87

[185] Ancestry.com, *Tennessee, Death Records*, 1908-1958, Ancestry.com Operations, Inc:2011, Tennessee State Library and Archives; Nashville, Tennessee; Tennessee Death Records, 1908-1959; Roll #:87

[186] Ancestry.com, *Tennessee, Death Records*, 1908-1958, Ancestry.com Operations, Inc:2011, Tennessee State Library and Archives; Nashville, Tennessee; Tennessee Death Records, 1908-1959; Roll #:87

## Sarah Jane "Sally" Futrell Bottomlee Family

**1.2.5 Sarah Jane "Sally" Futrell**[3] (*John E.*[2],

*Etheldred*[1]), daughter of John E. and Elizabeth Walls

Futrell, was born 21 March 1878 in Morgan County,

Tennessee.[187] She married Norris Lucas Bottomlee on 27

December 1897 in Morgan County.[188] Norris was

previously married to Lydia Hurt in Rhea County on 18

June 1887.[189] Sally and Norris are shown living in the

Eighth District of Rhea County in 1900.[190] They were living

in Coalfield by the birth of their son Leonard in April

1902,[191] living on Back Valley Road in 1920,[192] and then

moved to Letcher County, Kentucky before 1930.[193] Norris

died 11 April 1934 and was buried in the Frazier Cemetery

in Letcher County.[194] Sally died in Charleston, Kanawha,

---

[187] John E. Futrell Family Bible record

[188] Ancestry.com, Tennessee State Marriages, 1780-2002

[189] Ancestry.com, Tennessee State Marriages, 1780-2002

[190] Ancestry.com, *1900 United States Federal Census*, Ancestry.com Operations, Inc:2004, Year: 1900; Census Place: Civil District 8, Rhea, Tennessee; Roll: 1593; Page: 22A; Enumeration District: 0086; FHL microfilm: 1241593

[191] Ancestry.com, *Tennessee, Delayed Birth Records, 1869-1909*, Ancestry.com Operations, Inc:2012

[192] Ancestry.com, *1920 United States Federal Census*, Ancestry.com Operations, Inc:2010, Year: 1920; Census Place: Civil District 1, Morgan, Tennessee; Roll: T625_1758; Page: 16A; Enumeration District: 47; Image: 38

[193] Ancestry.com, *1930 United States Federal Census*, Ancestry.com Operations, Inc:2004, Year: 1930; Census Place: River, Letcher, Kentucky; Roll: 765; Page: 15B; Enumeration District: 0018; Image: 1000.0; FHL microfilm: 2340500

[194] Ancestry.com. *Web: Kentucky, Find A Grave Index, 1776-2012* [database on-line]. Provo, UT, USA: Ancestry.com Operations, Inc., 2012

West Virginia on 16 September 1949 and was also buried in the Frazier Cemetery in Letcher County.[195]

**1.2.5.1 Walter James Bottomlee**[4] (*Sarah Jane Futrell*[3], *John E.*[2], *Etheldred*[1]), son of Sally Futrell and Norris Bottomlee, was born on 7 July 1900 in Dayton, Rhea County, Tennessee.[196] The family was living in Coalfield in 1910[197] and 1920,[198] but Walter was living in Letcher County, Kentucky with his wife Artie Lee Frazier and two children by 1930 and working as a coal miner.[199] Walter died in Kanawha, West Virginia on 20 December 1956.[200] Artie died on 26 January 1994 in Racine, West Virginia.[201]

---

[195] Ancestry.com. *West Virginia, Deaths Index, 1853-1973* [database online]. Provo, UT, USA: Ancestry.com Operations, Inc., 2011

[196] Ancestry.com, *Tennessee, Delayed Birth Records, 1869-1909*, Ancestry.com Operations, Inc:2012

[197] Ancestry.com, *1910 United States Federal Census*, Ancestry.com Operations, Inc:1006, Year: 1910; Census Place: Civil District 1, Morgan, Tennessee; Roll: T624_1514; Page: 13B; Enumeration District: 0050; FHL microfilm: 1375527

[198] Ancestry.com, *1920 United States Federal Census*, Ancestry.com Operations, Inc:2010, Year: 1920; Census Place: Civil District 1, Morgan, Tennessee; Roll: T625_1758; Page: 16A; Enumeration District: 47; Image: 38

[199] Ancestry.com, *1930 United States Federal Census*, Ancestry.com Operations, Inc:2004, Year: 1930; Census Place: River, Letcher, Kentucky; Roll: 765; Page: 16B; Enumeration District: 0018; Image: 1002.0; FHL microfilm: 2340500

[200] Ancestry.com, *U.S., Social Security Death Index, 1935-2014*, Ancestry.com Operations, Inc:2011, Number: 235-10-7681; Issue State: West Virginia; Issue Date: Before 1951

[201] Ancestry.com, *U.S., Social Security Death Index, 1935-2014*, Ancestry.com Operations, Inc:2011, Number: 233-64-4247; Issue State: West Virginia; Issue Date: 1957

**1.2.5.2 Leonard Etheldred Bottomlee[4]** (*Sarah Jane Futrell[3], John E.[2], Etheldred[1]*), son of Sally Futrell and Norris Bottomlee, was born on 6 April 1902 in Coalfield, Morgan County, Tennessee.[202] The family moved to Letcher County, Kentucky by 1930 when Leonard still lived with his parents.[203] Leonard apparently married shortly thereafter, as he and his wife Josephine Blair were living in Pax, Fayette County, West Virginia with their six year old son in 1940.[204] Leonard died in Wyoming, West Virginia on 26 December 1946.[205]

**1.2.5.3 Minnie Jane Bottomlee[4]** (*Sarah Jane Futrell[3], John E.[2], Etheldred[1]*), daughter of Sally Futrell and Norris Bottomlee, was born on 27 July 1904 in Coalfield, Morgan County, Tennessee.[206] She lived with her parents on Back Valley Road in 1920.[207] Minnie was living in Letcher County, Kentucky with her husband Hibert

---

[202] Ancestry.com, *Tennessee, Delayed Birth Records, 1869-1909*, Ancestry.com Operations, Inc:2012
[203] Ancestry.com, *1930 United States Federal Census*, Ancestry.com Operations, Inc:2004, Year: 1930; Census Place: River, Letcher, Kentucky; Roll: 765; Page: 15B; Enumeration District: 0018; Image: 1000.0; FHL microfilm: 2340500
[204] Ancestry.com, *1940 United States Federal Census*, Ancestry.com Operations, Inc:2010, **Year: 1940; Census Place: Pax, Fayette, West Virginia; Roll: T627_4401; Page: 2A; Enumeration District: 10-10**
[205] Ancestry.com, *West Virginia, Deaths Index, 1853-1973*, Ancestry.com Operations, Inc:2011
[206] Ancestry.com, *Tennessee, Delayed Birth Records, 1869-1909*, Ancestry.com Operations, Inc:2012
[207] Ancestry.com, *1920 United States Federal Census*, Ancestry.com Operations, Inc:2010, Year: 1920; Census Place: Civil District 1, Morgan, Tennessee; Roll: T625_1758; Page: 16A; Enumeration District: 47; Image: 38

Dixon and two children in 1930.[208] Minnie and Hibert divorced before 1940 when she was found living as head of household in Whitesburg, Letcher County, Kentucky with her two sons.[209]

**1.2.5.4 Arnold Norris Bottomlee[4]** (*Sarah Jane Futrell[3], John E.[2], Etheldred[1]*), son of Sally Futrell and Norris Bottomlee, was born on 10 August 1906 in Coalfield, Morgan County, Tennessee.[210] He married Pauline Crist in Fayetteville, West Virginia on 6 November 1928.[211] They were living in Kanawha, Fayette County, West Virginia with two children in 1930 and Arnold's occupation was coal miner.[212] Pauline died on 31 July 1981 in Beckley, Raleigh County, West Virginia[213] and Arnold died five years later on 28 December 1986 in Beckley.[214] Both are buried in

---

[208] Ancestry.com, *1930 United States Federal Census*, Ancestry.com Operations, Inc:2004, Year: 1930; Census Place: River, Letcher, Kentucky; Roll: 765; Page: 15B; Enumeration District: 0018; Image: 1000.0; FHL microfilm: 2340500

[209] Ancestry.com, *1940 United States Federal Census*, Ancestry.com Operations, Inc:2010, Year: 1940; Census Place:Whitesburg, Letcher, Kentucky; Roll: T627_1330; Page: 12B; Enumeration District: 67-1

[210] Ancestry.com, *U.S., Find A Grave Index, 1600s-Current*, Ancestry.com Operations, Inc:2012

[211] Ancestry.com, *West Virginia, Marriages Index, 1785-1971*, Ancestry.com Operations, Inc.:2011

[212] Ancestry.com, *1930 United States Federal Census*, Ancestry.com Operations, Inc:2004, Year: 1930; Census Place: Kanawha, Fayette, West Virginia; Roll: 2531; Page: 9B; Enumeration District: 0025; Image: 452.0; FHL microfilm: 2342265

[213] Ancestry.com, *U.S., Find A Grave Index, 1600s-Current*, Ancestry.com Operations, Inc:2012

[214] Ancestry.com, *U.S., Find A Grave Index, 1600s-Current*, Ancestry.com Operations, Inc:2012

Palm Memorial Gardens in Matheny, Wyoming County, West Virginia.[215]

**1.2.5.5 Glenn Bottomlee**[4] (*Sarah Jane Futrell*[3], *John E.*[2], *Etheldred*[1]), son of Sally Futrell and Norris Bottomlee, was born about 1909 in Blue Gem (Coalhill), Morgan County, Tennessee. He died at the age of two on 13 May 1911 in Blue Gem.[216]

**1.2.5.6 Viola Mae Bottomlee**[4] (*Sarah Jane Futrell*[3], *John E.*[2], *Etheldred*[1]), daughter of Sally Futrell and Norris Bottomlee, was born on 28 October 1911 in Harriman, Roane County, Tennessee.[217] Viola lived with her parents in Letcher County, Kentucky in 1930,[218] and later married (Unknown) Frazier. Viola died on 2 September 1996 in Premium, Letcher County, Kentucky.[219]

**Stepchildren of Sarah Jane "Sally" Futrell Bottomlee**

---

[215] Ancestry.com, *U.S., Find A Grave Index, 1600s-Current*, Ancestry.com Operations, Inc:2012
[216] Ancestry.com, *Tennessee, Death Records*, 1908-1958, Ancestry.com Operations, Inc:2011, Tennessee State Library and Archives; Nashville, Tennessee; Tennessee Death Records, 1908-1959; Roll #: 23
[217] Ancestry.com, *U.S., Social Security Death Index, 1935-2014*, Ancestry.com Operations, Inc:2011, Number: 403-98-1313; Issue State: Kentucky; Issue Date: 1975
[218] Ancestry.com, *1930 United States Federal Census*, Ancestry.com Operations, Inc:2004, Year: 1930; Census Place: River, Letcher, Kentucky; Roll: 765; Page: 15B; Enumeration District: 0018; Image: 1000.0; FHL microfilm: 2340500
[219] Ancestry.com, *U.S., Social Security Death Index, 1935-2014*, Ancestry.com Operations, Inc:2011, Number: 403-98-1313; Issue State: Kentucky; Issue Date: 1975

Children of Norris Bottomlee and Lydia Hurt[220]

- Alexander F. Bottomlee
- Martha E. Bottomlee
- Lydia A. Bottomlee

## John Albert Futrell Family

**1.2.6 John Albert Futrell[3]** (*John E.[2], Etheldred[1]*), son of John E. and Elizabeth Walls Futrell, was born 29 November 1881 in Morgan County, Tennessee.[221] He married Martha E. Bottomlee on 26 December 1907 in Morgan County.[222] John died on 4 December 1961[223] and Martha died on 28 December 1967;[224] they are buried in the Coalhill Cemetery in Morgan County.[225]

**1.2.6.1 James Franklin Futrell[4]** (*John Albert[3], John E.[2], Etheldred[1]*), son of John Albert and Martha Bottomlee Futrell, was born 2 January 1909 in Morgan County, Tennessee.[226] He married Stella M. Clark on 23

[220] Ancestry.com, *1900 United States Federal Census*, Ancestry.com Operations, Inc:2004, Year: 1900; Census Place: Civil District 8, Rhea, Tennessee; Roll: 1593; Page: 22A; Enumeration District: 0086; FHL microfilm: 1241593
[221] John E. Futrell Family Bible record
[222] Ancestry.com, Tennessee State Marriages, 1780-2002
[223] Ancestry.com, *U.S., Find A Grave Index, 1600s-Current*, Ancestry.com Operations, Inc:2012
[224] Ancestry.com, *U.S., Find A Grave Index, 1600s-Current*, Ancestry.com Operations, Inc:2012
[225] Ancestry.com, *U.S., Find A Grave Index, 1600s-Current*, Ancestry.com Operations, Inc:2012
[226] Ancestry.com and Ohio Department of Health, *Ohio, Deaths, 1908-1932, 1938-2007*, Ancestry.com Operations, Inc:2010

December 1926 in Roane County.[227] James and Stella moved from Morgan County to Dayton, Ohio between 1940 and 1954.[228] James died 29 April 1987 in Dayton, Ohio[229] and Stella died in Dayton on 31 October 1992.[230]

**1.2.6.2 Susan Jane "Janie" Futrell[4]** (*John Albert[3], John E.[2], Etheldred[1]*), daughter of John Albert and Martha Bottomlee Futrell, was born 11 June 1911 in Morgan County, Tennessee.[231] She married Samuel B. Jones on 26 December 1926 in Anderson County.[232] After making their home at the corner of Lower Jackson and Cumberland Roads in Coalfield, they moved to Roane County around 1950.[233] Sam died on 1 August 1963[234] and Janie died 31 August 1976.[235] Both are buried in the Coalhill Cemetery in Morgan County.[236]

---

[227] Ancestry.com, Tennessee State Marriages, 1780-2002
[228] Ancestry.com, *1940 United States Federal Census*, Ancestry.com Operations, Inc:2010, **Year: 1940; Census Place: Morgan, Tennessee; Roll: T627_3924; Page: 19B; Enumeration District: 65-1**
[229] Ancestry.com and Ohio Department of Health, *Ohio, Deaths, 1908-1932, 1938-2007*, Ancestry.com Operations, Inc:2010
[230] Ancestry.com and Ohio Department of Health, *Ohio, Deaths, 1908-1932, 1938-2007*, Ancestry.com Operations, Inc:2010
[231] Ancestry.com, *U.S., Find A Grave Index, 1600s-Current*, Ancestry.com Operations, Inc:2012
[232] Ancestry.com, Tennessee State Marriages, 1780-2002
[233] Personal knowledge of author
[234] Ancestry.com, *U.S., Find A Grave Index, 1600s-Current*, Ancestry.com Operations, Inc:2012
[235] Ancestry.com, *U.S., Find A Grave Index, 1600s-Current*, Ancestry.com Operations, Inc:2012
[236] Ancestry.com, *U.S., Find A Grave Index, 1600s-Current*, Ancestry.com Operations, Inc:2012

**1.2.6.3 Edith Elizabeth Futrell**[4] (*John Albert*[3], *John E., Etheldred*), daughter of John Albert and Martha Bottomlee Futrell, was born 9 October 1914 in Morgan County, Tennessee.[237] She married James Arvel Clark on 1 March 1932 in Morgan County.[238] They moved from Coalfield to the Cincinnati, Ohio area after the death of their daughter Carolyn on 2 November 1948.[239] Edith died on 5 December 1999 in Cincinnati.[240] James died in Loveland, Ohio on 14 January 2007.[241] Both are buried in Reading, Ohio.[242]

**1.2.6.4 John Henry Futrell**[4] (*John Albert*[3], *John E.*[2], *Etheldred*[1]), son of John Albert and Martha Bottomlee Futrell, was born 8 December 1917 in Morgan County, Tennessee.[243] He married Mary E. Smith on 8 July, 1940 in Morgan County,[244] and moved to the Greenville, South Carolina area. Mary died on 25 January 1991[245] and John

---

[237] Ancestry.com, *U.S., Find A Grave Index, 1600s-Current*, Ancestry.com Operations, Inc:2012

[238] Ancestry.com, Tennessee State Marriages, 1780-2002

[239] Ancestry.com, *U.S., Find A Grave Index, 1600s-Current*, Ancestry.com Operations, Inc:2012

[240] Ancestry.com, *U.S., Find A Grave Index, 1600s-Current*, Ancestry.com Operations, Inc:2012

[241] Ancestry.com, *U.S., Find A Grave Index, 1600s-Current*, Ancestry.com Operations, Inc:2012

[242] Ancestry.com, *U.S., Find A Grave Index, 1600s-Current*, Ancestry.com Operations, Inc:2012

[243] Ancestry.com, *U.S., Find A Grave Index, 1600s-Current*, Ancestry.com Operations, Inc:2012

[244] Ancestry.com, Tennessee State Marriages, 1780-2002

[245] Ancestry.com, *U.S., Find A Grave Index, 1600s-Current*, Ancestry.com Operations, Inc:2012

Henry died on 29 December 2004 in Marietta, South Carolina.[246] Both are buried in the Jones Hill Church of God Cemetery in Pumpkintown, South Carolina.[247]

**1.2.6.5 Walter Hubert Futrell**[4] (*John Albert*[3], *John E.*[2], *Etheldred*[1]), son of John Albert and Martha Bottomlee Futrell, was born on 22 May 1930 in Roane County, Tennessee.[248] He married Peggy Manis on 6 August 1954 in Ringgold, Catoosa County, Georgia.[249] They made their home in Harriman, Roane County, and were eventually divorced in Roane County. Walter had already moved to another state, and eventually took residence in Greenville County, South Carolina where his brother John Henry resided. Walter died in Greenville on 26 January 1995 and was buried in the Coalhill Cemetery in Morgan County, Tennessee.[250]

## George W. Futrell

**1.2.7 George W. Futrell**[3] (*John E.*[2], *Etheldred*[1]), son of John E. and Elizabeth Walls Futrell, was born 21

[246] Web: www.legacy.com/obituaries/greenvilleonline/obituary.aspx?n=john-futrell&pid=140646923#sthash.ggwP0BQD.dpuf

[247] Ancestry.com, *U.S., Find A Grave Index, 1600s-Current*, Ancestry.com Operations, Inc:2012

[248] Kyker Funeral Home of Harriman, Tennessee Death Index, Volume II, McMinn County Historical Society and Archives:2005

[249] Kyker Funeral Home of Harriman, Tennessee Death Index, Volume II, McMinn County Historical Society and Archives:2005

[250] Ancestry.com, *U.S., Find A Grave Index, 1600s-Current*, Ancestry.com Operations, Inc:2012

February 1885 in Morgan County.[251] Other than the date of birth found in John Futrell's family Bible, no record has been found of George's existence. He is not included in the 1900 census at which time he would have been only 15 years old and presumably at home. It is assumed that George died before 1900.

---

[251] John E. Futrell Family Bible record

# Generations 3 and 4: Descendants of Noah Alexander Futrell

## Etheldred T. Futrell Family

**1.3.1 Etheldred T. Futrell**[3] *(Noah Alexander*[2]*, Etheldred*[1]*)*, son of Noah Alexander and Sarafina Edwards Futrell, was born 28 January 1869 in Roane County, Tennessee.[252] He lived with his father Noah in Civil District 14 of Roane County in 1900.[253] Shortly thereafter he married Ether Peters on 25 October 1900 in Roane County.[254] By 1910, Etheldred and Ether lived with three children in Civil District 2 of Roane County.[255] They lived in the same location in 1920 with four children.[256] In 1930, their address is listed as Hen Valley Road in District 2[257]

---

[252] Ancestry.com, Tennessee, Death Records, 1908-1958, Ancestry.com Operations, Inc.:2011, Tennessee State Library and Archives; Nashville, Tennessee; Tennessee Death Records, 1908-1959

[253] Ancestry.com, *1900 United States Federal Census*, Ancestry.com Operations, Inc:2004, Year: 1900; Census Place: Civil District 14, Roane, Tennessee; Roll: 1593; Page: 19B; Enumeration District: 0116; FHL microfilm: 1241593

[254] Ancestry.com, Tennessee State Marriages, 1780-2002

[255] Ancestry.com, *1910 United States Federal Census*, Ancestry.com Operations, Inc:2006, Year: 1910; Census Place: Oliver Springs, Roane, Tennessee; Roll: T624_1517; Page: 5A; Enumeration District: 0150; FHL microfilm: 1375530

[256] Ancestry.com, *1920 United States Federal Census*, Ancestry.com Operations, Inc:2010, Year: 1920; Census Place: Civil District 2, Roane, Tennessee; Roll: T625_1760; Page: 7B; Enumeration District: 161; Image: 817

[257] Ancestry.com, *1930 United States Federal Census*, Ancestry.com Operations, Inc:2002, Year: 1930; Census Place: District 2, Roane, Tennessee; Roll: 2269; Page: 3A; Enumeration District: 0006; Image: 747.0; FHL microfilm: 2342003

and in 1940 their address is listed as Hannah Highway.[258]
Etheldred died 23 January 1952 in Harriman, Roane
County.[259] Ether died 24 August 1962.[260] Both are buried
in the Elverton Cemetery in Roane County.[261]

**1.3.1.1 Eric Brant Futrell**[4] *(Etheldred T.[3], Noah
Alexander[2], Etheldred[1])*, son of Etheldred T. and Ether
Peters Futrell, was born 2 June 1903, presumably in Roane
County, Tennessee. Eric died a few weeks later on 28 July
1903 and is buried in the Edwards Cemetery in Roane
County.[262] While no documentation can be found for Eric's
parental relationship, Noah was widowed before 1900 and
Etheldred T. Futrell is the only logical possibility.

**1.3.1.1 Ellery Ordwell Futrell**[4] *(Etheldred T.[3],
Noah Alexander[2], Etheldred[1])*, son of Etheldred T. and
Ether Peters Futrell, was born 1 July 1904 in Harriman,
Roane County, Tennessee.[263] He married Georgia M.
Braden on 27 October 1928 in Campbell County,

---

[258] Ancestry.com, *1940 United States Federal Census*, Ancestry.com
Operations, Inc:2012, Year: 1940; **Census Place: Roane, Tennessee; Roll:
T627_3929; Page: 6B; Enumeration District: 73-9**
[259] Ancestry.com, Tennessee, Death Records, 1908-1958, Ancestry.com
Operations, Inc.:2011, Tennessee State Library and Archives; Nashville,
Tennessee; Tennessee Death Records, 1908-1959
[260] Ancestry.com, *U.S., Find A Grave Index, 1600s-Current*,
Ancestry.com Operations, Inc:2012
[261] Ancestry.com, *U.S., Find A Grave Index, 1600s-Current*,
Ancestry.com Operations, Inc:2012
[262] Ancestry.com, *U.S., Find A Grave Index, 1600s-Current*,
Ancestry.com Operations, Inc:2012
[263] Ancestry.com, *Tennessee, Delayed Birth Records, 1869-1909*,
Ancestry.com Operations, Inc:2012

Tennessee.[264] In 1930, they lived on Hen Valley Road in Roane County with their newborn son.[265] By 1940 they lived on Hannah Highway in Roane County with three children.[266] Ellery died on 20 January 1978 in Oak Ridge, Tennessee and was buried in Oak Ridge Memorial Park.[267]

**1.3.1.2 Noah A. Futrell[4]** *(Etheldred T.[3], Noah Alexander[2], Etheldred[1])*, son of Etheldred T. and Ether Peters Futrell, was born with his twin brother Elijah on 25 May 1908 in Roane County, Tennessee.[268] Noah died on 29 November 1983 in Harriman, Roane County.[269] He is buried in the Elverton Cemetery in Roane County.[270]

**1.3.1.3 Elijah W. Futrell[4]** *(Etheldred T.[3], Noah Alexander[2], Etheldred[1])*, son of Etheldred T. and Ether Peters Futrell, was born with his twin brother Noah on 25

---

[264] Ancestry.com, Tennessee State Marriages, 1780-2002

[265] Ancestry.com, *1930 United States Federal Census*, Ancestry.com Operations, Inc:2002, Year: 1930; Census Place: District 2, Roane, Tennessee; Roll: 2269; Page: 3A; Enumeration District: 0006; Image: 747.0; FHL microfilm: 2342003

[266] Ancestry.com, *1940 United States Federal Census*, Ancestry.com Operations, Inc:2012, Year: 1940; **Census Place: Roane, Tennessee; Roll: T627_3929; Page: 7A; Enumeration District: 73-9**

[267] Ancestry.com, *U.S., Social Security Death Index, 1935-2014*, Ancestry.com Operations, Inc:2011, Number: 411-14-6312; Issue State: Tennessee; Issue Date: Before 1951

[268] Ancestry.com, *U.S., Social Security Death Index, 1935-2014*, Ancestry.com Operations, Inc:2011, Number: 414-08-3214; Issue State: Tennessee; Issue Date: 1973

[269] Ancestry.com, *U.S., Social Security Death Index, 1935-2014*, Ancestry.com Operations, Inc:2011, Number: 414-08-3214; Issue State: Tennessee; Issue Date: 1973

[270] Ancestry.com, *U.S., Find A Grave Index, 1600s-Current*, Ancestry.com Operations, Inc:2012

May 1908 in Roane County, Tennessee.[271] Elijah died on 28
May 1981 in Harriman, Roane County.[272] He is buried in
the Elverton Cemetery in Roane County.[273]

**1.3.1.4 Dora Futrell**[4] *(Etheldred T.*[3]*, Noah
Alexander*[2]*, Etheldred*[1]*)*, daughter of Etheldred T. and
Ether Peters Futrell, was born on 22 June 1913 in Roane
County, Tennessee.[274] She married Luther Alexander
Bagwell on 5 October 1928 in Roane County.[275] In 1940
Dora and Luther lived on Hannah Highway in Roane
County with four children.[276] Luther died in Chatsworth,
Georgia on 20 June 1984 and is buried in the Coalhill
Cemetery in Morgan County, Tennessee.[277] Dora died in

---

[271] Ancestry.com, *U.S., Social Security Death Index, 1935-2014*,
Ancestry.com Operations, Inc:2011, Number: 415-07-1914; Issue State:
Tennessee; Issue Date: Before 1951
[272] Ancestry.com, *U.S., Social Security Death Index, 1935-2014*,
Ancestry.com Operations, Inc:2011, Number: 415-07-1914; Issue State:
Tennessee; Issue Date: Before 1951
[273] Ancestry.com, *U.S., Find A Grave Index, 1600s-Current*,
Ancestry.com Operations, Inc:2012
[274] Ancestry.com, *U.S., Social Security Death Index, 1935-2014*,
Ancestry.com Operations, Inc:2011, Number: 408-44-2085; Issue State:
Tennessee; Issue Date: Before 1951
[275] Ancestry.com, Tennessee State Marriages, 1780-2002
[276] Ancestry.com, *1940 United States Federal Census*, Ancestry.com
Operations, Inc:2012, Year: 1940; **Census Place: Roane, Tennessee; Roll:
T627_3929; Page: 7A; Enumeration District: 73-9**
[277] Ancestry.com, *U.S., Social Security Death Index, 1935-2014*,
Ancestry.com Operations, Inc:2011, Number: 415-07-1489; Issue State:
Tennessee; Issue Date: Before 1951

Harriman, Roane County on 28 April 1986 and is buried in the Elverton Cemetery in Roane County.[278]

## Malinda Ann Futrell Mayton Family

**1.3.2 Malinda Ann Futrell[3]** *(Noah[2], Etheldred[1])*, daughter of Noah Alexander and Sarafina Edwards Futrell, was born 14 August 1871 in Roane County, Tennessee.[279] She married Alexander Mayton on 30 December 1894 in Roane County.[280] The 1910 census shows them living in Oliver Springs with five children.[281] Malinda died 12 August 1915 in Swan Pond, Roane County.[282] Alexander died on 10 August 1921 in Harriman, Roane County.[283] Both are buried in the Dyllis Church Cemetery in Roane County.[284]

---

[278] Ancestry.com, *U.S., Social Security Death Index, 1935-2014*, Ancestry.com Operations, Inc:2011, Number: 408-44-2085; Issue State: Tennessee; Issue Date: Before 1951

[279] Ancestry.com, *1940 United States Federal Census*, Ancestry.com Operations, Inc:2012, Year: 1940; **Census Place: Roane, Tennessee; Roll: T627_3929; Page: 6B; Enumeration District: 73-9, Roll #: 39**

[280] Ancestry.com, Tennessee State Marriages, 1780-2002

[281] Ancestry.com, *1910 United States Federal Census*, Ancestry.com Operations, Inc:2006, Year: 1910; Census Place: Oliver Springs, Roane, Tennessee; Roll: T624_1517; Page: 1A; Enumeration District: 0150; FHL microfilm: 1375530

[282] Ancestry.com, *1940 United States Federal Census*, Ancestry.com Operations, Inc:2012, Year: 1940; **Census Place: Roane, Tennessee; Roll: T627_3929; Page: 6B; Enumeration District: 73-9, Roll #: 39**

[283] Ancestry.com, Tennessee, Death Records, 1908-1958, Ancestry.com Operations, Inc.:2011, Tennessee State Library and Archives; Nashville, Tennessee; Tennessee Death Records, 1908-1959, Roll #: 131

[284] Ancestry.com, *U.S., Find A Grave Index, 1600s-Current*, Ancestry.com Operations, Inc:2012

**1.3.2.1 Sarah Elizabeth Mayton**[4] *(Malinda Ann Futrell*[3]*, Noah Alexander*[2]*, Etheldred*[1]*)*, daughter of Alexander and Malinda Ann Futrell Mayton, was born on 5 September 1895 in Roane County, Tennessee.[285] She married Richmond S. Baker on 16 December 1922 in Roane County.[286] The 1930 census shows them living in Precinct 6, Tarrant, Texas with one child and two of Sarah's brothers in the household.[287] In 1940 Sarah and Richmond lived in Bradley County, Tennessee with their daughter.[288] Sarah died on 17 October 1957 in Cleveland, Bradley County.[289] Richmond died on 24 April 1961 in Cleveland. Both are buried in the Fort Hill Cemetery in Cleveland.[290]

**1.3.2.2 Maggie Carolyn Mayton**[4] *(Malinda Ann Futrell*[3]*, Noah Alexander*[2]*, Etheldred*[1]*)*, daughter of Alexander and Malinda Ann Futrell Mayton, was born 13

---

[285] Ancestry.com, Tennessee, Death Records, 1908-1958, Ancestry.com Operations, Inc.:2011, Tennessee State Library and Archives; Nashville, Tennessee; Tennessee Death Records, 1908-1959

[286] Ancestry.com, Tennessee State Marriages, 1780-2002

[287] Ancestry.com, *1930 United States Federal Census*, Ancestry.com Operations, Inc:2002, Year: 1930; Census Place: Precinct 6, Tarrant, Texas; Roll: 2399; Page: 3A; Enumeration District: 0121; Image: 41.0; FHL microfilm: 2342133

[288] Ancestry.com, *1940 United States Federal Census*, Ancestry.com Operations, Inc:2012, Year: 1940; **Census Place: Bradley, Tennessee; Roll: T627_3875; Page: 18B; Enumeration District: 6-17**

[289] Ancestry.com, Tennessee, Death Records, 1908-1958, Ancestry.com Operations, Inc.:2011, Tennessee State Library and Archives; Nashville, Tennessee; Tennessee Death Records, 1908-1959

[290] Web: www.findagrave.com/cgi-bin/fg.cgi?page=gr&GRid=39704926&ref=acom

December 1897 in Roane County, Tennessee.[291] She married Floyd Campbell Andrew on 6 February 1916 in Roane County.[292] They lived in District 3 of Roane County near Kingston throughout their lives. Maggie died on 28 December 1944 in District 3 and was buried in the Poplar Springs Cemetery.[293] Floyd died on 14 May 1985 and is buried in the same cemetery.[294]

**1.3.2.3 Dora Ellen Mayton**[4] *(Malinda Ann Futrell³, Noah Alexander², Etheldred¹)*, daughter of Alexander and Malinda Ann Futrell Mayton, was born 22 November 1901 in Roane County, Tennessee.[295] She married Elder Elden Howard on 21 October 1922 in Roane County.[296] Both the 1930[297] and 1940 censuses show them living in Swan Pond in Roane County.[298] Elder died in

---

[291] Ancestry.com, Tennessee, Death Records, 1908-1958, Ancestry.com Operations, Inc.:2011, Tennessee State Library and Archives; Nashville, Tennessee; Tennessee Death Records, 1908-1959, Roll #: 12

[292] Ancestry.com, Tennessee State Marriages, 1780-2002

[293] Ancestry.com, Tennessee, Death Records, 1908-1958, Ancestry.com Operations, Inc.:2011, Tennessee State Library and Archives; Nashville, Tennessee; Tennessee Death Records, 1908-1959, Roll #: 12

[294] Ancestry.com, *U.S., Find A Grave Index, 1600s-Current*, Ancestry.com Operations, Inc:2012

[295] Ancestry.com, *Tennessee, Delayed Birth Records, 1869-1909*, Ancestry.com Operations, Inc:2012

[296] Ancestry.com, Tennessee State Marriages, 1780-2002

[297] Ancestry.com, *1930 United States Federal Census*, Ancestry.com Operations, Inc:2002, Year: 1930; Census Place: District 1, Roane, Tennessee; Roll: 2269; Page: 13A; Enumeration District: 0003; Image: 677.0; FHL microfilm: 2342003

[298] Ancestry.com, *1940 United States Federal Census*, Ancestry.com Operations, Inc:2012, Year: 1940; **Census Place: Roane, Tennessee; Roll: T627_3929; Page: 6B; Enumeration District: 73-5**

Harriman, Roane County on 23 November 1994.[299] Dora died on 5 April 1996 in Dayton, Montgomery County, Ohio.[300]

**1.3.2.4 Andrew Jack Mayton**[4] *(Malinda Ann Futrell[3], Noah Alexander[2], Etheldred[1])*, son of Alexander and Malinda Ann Futrell Mayton, was born 14 October 1905 in Tennessee.[301] He married Teresa McKinney on 25 October 1924 in Roane County, Tennessee.[302] Teresa died on 10 August 1926 of tuberculosis.[303] The 1930 census shows Jack living in the household of his sister and brother-in-law in Precinct 6, Tarrant, Texas.[304] Jack died at the age of 25 in Tarrant on 9 November 1930, also from tuberculosis.[305]

**1.3.2.5 Walter Mayton**[4] *(Malinda Ann Futrell[3], Noah Alexander[2], Etheldred[1])*, son of Alexander and

---

[299] Ancestry.com, *U.S., Social Security Death Index, 1935-2014*, Ancestry.com Operations, Inc:2011, Number: 254-12-9306; Issue State: Georgia; Issue Date: Before 1951

[300] Ancestry.com, *U.S., Social Security Death Index, 1935-2014*, Ancestry.com Operations, Inc:2011, Number: 408-01-3035; Issue State: Tennessee; Issue Date: Before 1951

[301] Ancestry.com, *Texas, Death Certificates, 1903–1982*, Ancestry.com Operations, Inc:2013

[302] Ancestry.com, Tennessee State Marriages, 1780-2002

[303] Ancestry.com, Tennessee, Death Records, 1908-1958, Ancestry.com Operations, Inc.:2011, Tennessee State Library and Archives; Nashville, Tennessee; Tennessee Death Records, 1908-1959, Roll #: 9

[304] Ancestry.com, *1930 United States Federal Census*, Ancestry.com Operations, Inc:2002, Year: 1930; Census Place: Precinct 6, Tarrant, Texas; Roll: 2399; Page: 3A; Enumeration District: 0121; Image: 41.0; FHL microfilm: 2342133

[305] Ancestry.com, *Texas, Death Certificates, 1903–1982*, Ancestry.com Operations, Inc:2013

Malinda Ann Futrell Mayton, was born 28 November 1908 in Roane County, Tennessee.[306] The 1930 census shows Walter living in the household of his sister and brother-in-law in Precinct 6, Tarrant, Texas.[307] Walter married Bonnie M. (Unknown).[308] Walter moved to Cleveland, Bradley County, Tennessee by 1949[309] where his sister and her husband also relocated from Texas. Walter and Bonnie both died on 1 January 1974[310, 311] and are buried in Sunset Memorial Gardens in Cleveland.[312]

## Elizabeth "Betty" Jane Futrell Mullins Family

**1.3.3 Elizabeth "Betty" Jane Futrell**[3] *(Noah², Etheldred¹)*, daughter of Noah Alexander and Sarafina Edwards Futrell, was born 25 February 1875 in Roane County, Tennessee.[313] She married Frank W. Mullins on 1 October 1893 in Roane County.[314] The 1910 census shows

[306] Ancestry.com, *Tennessee, Delayed Birth Records, 1869-1909*, Ancestry.com Operations, Inc:2012

[307] Ancestry.com, *1930 United States Federal Census*, Ancestry.com Operations, Inc:2002, Year: 1930; Census Place: Precinct 6, Tarrant, Texas; Roll: 2399; Page: 3A; Enumeration District: 0121; Image: 41.0; FHL microfilm: 2342133

[308] Ancestry.com, *U.S., Find A Grave Index, 1600s-Current*, Ancestry.com Operations, Inc:2012

[309] Ancestry.com, **U.S. City Directories, 1822-1989**, Ancestry.com Operations, Inc:2011

[310] Web: http://www.locateancestors.com/mayton-tennessee/

[311] Web: http://www.locateancestors.com/mayton-tennessee/

[312] Ancestry.com, *U.S., Find A Grave Index, 1600s-Current*, Ancestry.com Operations, Inc:2012

[313] Ancestry.com, Tennessee, Death Records, 1908-1958, Ancestry.com Operations, Inc.:2011, Tennessee State Library and Archives; Nashville, Tennessee; Tennessee Death Records, 1908-1959, Roll #: 13

[314] Ancestry.com, Tennessee State Marriages, 1780-2002

them living in Civil District 14 of Roane County.[315] Later censuses in 1920[316] and 1930[317] show them living in Civil District 1 of Roane County. Frank died 2 February 1930 in Harriman, Roane County[318] and is buried in the Edwards Cemetery in Sugar Grove, Roane County.[319] Betty died 19 September 1948 in Harriman[320] and is buried in the Elverton Cemetery in Roane County.[321]

**1.3.3.1 Off Mullins[4]** *(Elizabeth Jane Futrell[3], Noah Alexander[2], Etheldred[1])*, son of Frank W. and Elizabeth "Betty" Jane Futrell Mullins, was born 4 June 1894 in Roane County, Tennessee.[322] He married Myrtle P.

---

[315] Ancestry.com, *1910 United States Federal Census*, Ancestry.com Operations, Inc:2006, Year: 1910; Census Place: Civil District 1, Roane, Tennessee; Roll: T624_1517; Page: 1A; Enumeration District: 0144; FHL microfilm: 1375530

[316] Ancestry.com, *1920 United States Federal Census*, Ancestry.com Operations, Inc:2010, Year: 1920; Census Place: Civil District 1, Roane, Tennessee; Roll: T625_1760; Page: 1A; Enumeration District: 156; Image: 628

[317] Ancestry.com, *1930 United States Federal Census*, Ancestry.com Operations, Inc:2002, Year: 1930; Census Place: District 1, Roane, Tennessee; Roll: 2269; Page: 2B; Enumeration District: 0003; Image: 656.0; FHL microfilm: 2342003

[318] Ancestry.com, Tennessee, Death Records, 1908-1958, Ancestry.com Operations, Inc.:2011, Tennessee State Library and Archives; Nashville, Tennessee; Tennessee Death Records, 1908-1959, Roll #: 2

[319] Ancestry.com, *U.S., Find A Grave Index, 1600s-Current*, Ancestry.com Operations, Inc:2012

[320] Ancestry.com, Tennessee, Death Records, 1908-1958, Ancestry.com Operations, Inc.:2011, Tennessee State Library and Archives; Nashville, Tennessee; Tennessee Death Records, 1908-1959, Roll #: 13

[321] Ancestry.com, *U.S., Find A Grave Index, 1600s-Current*, Ancestry.com Operations, Inc:2012

[322] Ancestry.com, *U.S., Social Security Death Index, 1935-2014*, Ancestry.com Operations, Inc:2011, Number: 409-09-2956; Issue State: Tennessee; Issue Date: Before 1951

Adkissin on 23 August 1914 in Roane County.[323] They lived
in District 1 of Roane County in 1930.[324] The couple
apparently divorced between 1930 and 1940 when Off is
found living with Bertha Ward and two young children in
Civil District 4 of Hamilton County, Tennessee.[325] Bertha
was previously married to John Harness[326] with whom she
had seven children. Off and Bertha were married on 22
May 1942 in Bradley County, Tennessee with a Birchwood,
Tennessee address.[327] Off died on 25 December 1967 and
Bertha died on 19 October 1969. Both are buried in the
Elverton Cemetery in Roane County.[328]

### 1.3.3.2 Matilda "Tilda" Melinda Mullins[4]

*(Elizabeth Jane Futrell[3], Noah Alexander[2], Etheldred[1])*,
daughter of Frank W. and Elizabeth "Betty" Jane Futrell
Mullins, was born 16 April 1896[329], presumably in Roane
County, Tennessee. She married George Washington
Taylor on 23 November 1914 in Morgan County,

---

[323] Ancestry.com, Tennessee State Marriages, 1780-2002
[324] Ancestry.com, *1930 United States Federal Census*, Ancestry.com
Operations, Inc:2002, Year: 1930; Census Place: District 1, Roane,
Tennessee; Roll: 2269; Page: 3A; Enumeration District: 0003; Image:
657.0; FHL microfilm: 2342003
[325] Ancestry.com, *1940 United States Federal Census*, Ancestry.com
Operations, Inc:2012, Year: 1940; Census Place: Hamilton, Tennessee;
Roll: T627_3899; Page: 8A; Enumeration District: 33-32
[326] Ancestry.com, Tennessee State Marriages, 1780-2002
[327] Ancestry.com, Tennessee State Marriages, 1780-2002
[328] Ancestry.com, *U.S., Find A Grave Index, 1600s-Current*,
Ancestry.com Operations, Inc:2012
[329] Ancestry.com, *U.S., Social Security Death Index, 1935-2014*,
Ancestry.com Operations, Inc:2011, Number: 415-07-1187; Issue State:
Tennessee; Issue Date: Before 1951

Tennessee[330]. The 1930 census shows them living in District 1 of Roane County[331]. Matilda died 15 September 1972 and is buried in the Elverton Cemetery in Roane County[332]. Note that the birth and death dates on her gravestone do not match those in the official Social Security death index.

**1.3.3.3 Sarah T. Mullins[4]** *(Elizabeth Jane Futrell[3], Noah Alexander[2], Etheldred[1])*, daughter of Frank W. and Elizabeth "Betty" Jane Futrell Mullins, was born 30 September 1899[333], presumably in Roane County, Tennessee. She married Virgil Hutsel Peters on 2 May 1915 in Roane County[334]. Sarah and Virgil lived in District 1 of Roane County[335]. Virgil died on 20 May, 1960[336] and

---

[330] Ancestry.com, Tennessee State Marriages, 1780-2002
[331] Ancestry.com, *1930 United States Federal Census*, Ancestry.com Operations, Inc:2002, Year: 1930; Census Place: District 1, Roane, Tennessee; Roll: 2269; Page: 3A; Enumeration District: 0003; Image: 657.0; FHL microfilm: 2342003
[332] Gravestone inscription in Elverton Cemetery, Roane, Tennessee, USA
[333] Ancestry.com, *U.S., Social Security Death Index, 1935-2014*, Ancestry.com Operations, Inc:2011, Number: 410-08-2014; Issue State: Tennessee; Issue Date: 1973
[334] Ancestry.com, Tennessee State Marriages, 1780-2002
[335] Ancestry.com, *1940 United States Federal Census*, Ancestry.com Operations, Inc:2012, Year: 1940; **Census Place: Roane, Tennessee; Roll: T627_3929; Page: 15B; Enumeration District: 73-5**
[336] Ancestry.com, *U.S., Find A Grave Index, 1600s-Current*, Ancestry.com Operations, Inc:2012

Sarah died on 30 December 1979[337]. Both are buried in the Elverton Cemetery in Roane County[338].

**1.3.3.4 Noah T. Mullins**[4] *(Elizabeth Jane Futrell[3], Noah Alexander[2], Etheldred[1])*, son of Frank W. and Elizabeth "Betty" Jane Futrell Mullins, was born 23 May 1902 in Harriman, Roane County, Tennessee.[339] No record was found of a marriage. Noah continued to live in District 1 of Roane County[340] and died 14 April 1980.[341] He is buried in the Elverton Cemetery in Roane County beside his sister Stella May Mullins.[342]

**1.3.3.5 Stella May Mullins**[4] *(Elizabeth Jane Futrell[3], Noah Alexander[2], Etheldred[1])*, daughter of Frank W. and Elizabeth "Betty" Jane Futrell Mullins, was born in 1904[343], presumably in Roane County, Tennessee. No record was found of a marriage. Stella continued to live in

---

[337] Ancestry.com, *U.S., Find A Grave Index, 1600s-Current*, Ancestry.com Operations, Inc:2012

[338] Ancestry.com, *U.S., Find A Grave Index, 1600s-Current*, Ancestry.com Operations, Inc:2012

[339] Ancestry.com, *U.S., Social Security Death Index, 1935-2014*, Ancestry.com Operations, Inc:2011, Number: 412-16-5236; Issue State: Tennessee; Issue Date: Before 1951

[340] Ancestry.com, *1930 United States Federal Census*, Ancestry.com Operations, Inc:2002, Year: 1930; Census Place: District 1, Roane, Tennessee; Roll: 2269; Page: 2B; Enumeration District: 0003; Image: 656.0; FHL microfilm: 2342003

[341] Ancestry.com, *U.S., Find A Grave Index, 1600s-Current*, Ancestry.com Operations, Inc:2012

[342] Ancestry.com, *U.S., Find A Grave Index, 1600s-Current*, Ancestry.com Operations, Inc:2012

[343] Ancestry.com, *U.S., Find A Grave Index, 1600s-Current*, Ancestry.com Operations, Inc:2012

the household of her mother and brother in District 1 of Roane County[344]. She died in 1962 and is buried in the Elverton Cemetery in Roane County beside her brother Noah T. Mullins[345].

**1.3.3.6 William Frank Mullins**[4] *(Elizabeth Jane Futrell[3], Noah Alexander[2], Etheldred[1])*, son of Frank W. and Elizabeth "Betty" Jane Futrell Mullins, was born 2 October 1907 in Harriman, Roane County, Tennessee[346]. He later married Ruth Kate Phillips (marriage date and location unknown)[347]. The 1940 census shows them living in District 1 of Roane County[348]. William died on 26 January 1947[349]. Ruth died on 29 September 1994[350]. Both are buried in the Dyllis Church Cemetery in Roane County[351].

---

[344] Ancestry.com, *1930 United States Federal Census*, Ancestry.com Operations, Inc:2002, Year: 1930; Census Place: District 1, Roane, Tennessee; Roll: 2269; Page: 2B; Enumeration District: 0003; Image: 656.0; FHL microfilm: 2342003
[345] Ancestry.com, *U.S., Find A Grave Index, 1600s-Current*, Ancestry.com Operations, Inc:2012
[346] Ancestry.com, *U.S., Find A Grave Index, 1600s-Current*, Ancestry.com Operations, Inc:2012
[347] Ancestry.com, *U.S., Find A Grave Index, 1777-2012*, Ancestry.com Operations, Inc:2012, Obituary of Mack James Mullins
[348] Ancestry.com, *1940 United States Federal Census*, Ancestry.com Operations, Inc:2012, Year: 1940; **Census Place: Roane, Tennessee; Roll: T627_3929; Page: 16A; Enumeration District: 73-5**
[349] Ancestry.com, *U.S., Find A Grave Index, 1600s-Current*, Ancestry.com Operations, Inc:2012
[350] Ancestry.com, *U.S., Find A Grave Index, 1600s-Current*, Ancestry.com Operations, Inc:2012
[351] Ancestry.com, *U.S., Find A Grave Index, 1600s-Current*, Ancestry.com Operations, Inc:2012

**1.3.3.7 Versia Mullins**[4] *(Elizabeth Jane Futrell[3], Noah Alexander[2], Etheldred[1])*, daughter of Frank W. and Elizabeth "Betty" Jane Futrell Mullins, was born 31 March 1910 in Tennessee[352], presumably in Roane County. She married William Howard on 12 May 1934 in Roane County[353] and they made their home in District 1 of Roane County[354]. Versia died 2 August 1981 while living in the Clax Gap community of Roane County and is buried in the Elverton Cemetery in Roane County[355].

**1.3.3.8 Reese Orey Mullins**[4] *(Elizabeth Jane Futrell[3], Noah Alexander[2], Etheldred[1])*, son of Frank W. and Elizabeth "Betty" Jane Futrell Mullins, was born 9 June 1914 in Tennessee[356], presumably in Roane County. He married Helen Margaret Howard on 8 April 1939 in Roane County[357] where they made their home[358]. Reese

---

[352] Ancestry.com, *U.S., Social Security Death Index, 1935-2014*, Ancestry.com Operations, Inc:2011, Number: 414-03-3046; Issue State: Tennessee; Issue Date: Before 1951

[353] Ancestry.com, Tennessee State Marriages, 1780-2002

[354] Ancestry.com, *1930 United States Federal Census*, Ancestry.com Operations, Inc:2002, Year: 1930; Census Place: District 1, Roane, Tennessee; Roll: 2269; Page: 2B; Enumeration District: 0003; Image: 656.0; FHL microfilm: 2342003

[355] *Versia Mullins Howard Obituary*, Roane County Heritage Center and Archives

[356] Ancestry.com, *U.S., Social Security Death Index, 1935-2014*, Ancestry.com Operations, Inc:2011, Number: 410-05-4315; Issue State: Tennessee; Issue Date: Before 1951

[357] Ancestry.com, Tennessee State Marriages, 1780-2002

[358] Ancestry.com, *1940 United States Federal Census*, Ancestry.com Operations, Inc:2012, Year: 1940; **Census Place: Roane, Tennessee; Roll: T627_3929; Page: 10B; Enumeration District: 73-5**

died 19 October 1978 in Harriman, Roane County[359]. Helen died on 31 December 2003[360]. Both are buried in Roane Memorial Gardens, Roane County[361].

---

[359] Kyker Funeral Home of Harriman, Tennessee Death Index, Volume II, McMinn County Historical Society and Archives:2005

[360] Ancestry.com, *U.S., Find A Grave Index, 1600s-Current*, Ancestry.com Operations, Inc:2012

[361] Ancestry.com, *U.S., Find A Grave Index, 1600s-Current*, Ancestry.com Operations, Inc:2012

# Outline Descendant Report
# for Etheldred Futrell

1 Etheldred Futrell b: 01 Aug 1800 in North Carolina, d: 29 Mar
   1884 in Morgan, Tennessee
...... + Sarah Martin b: 1808 in Tennessee, m: 1837 in Knox,
      Tennessee, d: 1851 in Knox, Tennessee
............2 Mary A. Futrell b: Abt. 1843 in Knox, Tennessee
............ + J L Baker m: 04 Nov 1862 in Knox, Tennessee
............2 John E. Futrell b: 01 Dec 1844 in Knox, Tennessee, d:
         23 Nov 1917 in Coalfield, Morgan, Tennessee
............ + Mary Elizabeth Walls b: 13 Feb 1843 in Knox,
         Tennessee, m: 24 Dec 1865 in Morgan, Tennessee, d:
         1913 in Morgan, Tennessee
.................3 Anna Elizabeth Futrell b: 06 Mar 1867 in Morgan,
         Tennessee, d: 1907
................. + William John "Bill" Overton b: 31 Aug 1861 in
            Loudon, Tennessee, m: 25 Sep 1897 in Morgan,
            Tennessee, d: 26 Feb 1909 in Lawnville, Roane,
            Tennessee
.......................4 Lucy Elizabeth Overton b: 17 Aug 1898 in
               Tennessee, d: 10 Dec 1934 in Harriman, Roane,
               Tennessee
....................... + George Thomas Poland b: 30 Aug 1893 in
               Harriman, Roane, Tennessee, m: 15 Feb 1918
               in Roane, Tennessee, d: 11 Oct 1953 in
               Harriman, Roane, Tennessee

.....................4 Margaret Robbie Overton b: 02 Nov 1899 in
Lawnville, Roane, Tennessee, d: 13 Apr 1991 in
Harriman, Roane, Tennessee

....................... + James Harvey Harmon b: 21 Oct 1894 in
Tennessee, m: 07 Nov 1924 in Roane,
Tennessee, d: 05 May 1956 in Harriman,
Roane, Tennessee

.....................4 John William Overton, Jr b: 26 Apr 1901 in
Tennessee, d: 10 Feb 1954 in Johnson City,
Washington, Tennessee

....................... + Willie Frank Wilson m: 14 Jun 1924 in Carter,
Tennessee

....................... + Loula Bertha Cassada b: 02 Jul 1896 in
Pulaski, KY, m: 12 Nov 1922 in Morgan,
Tennessee, d: 01 Jan 1929 in Harriman, Roane,
Tennessee

....................... + Louise Dixon b: Abt. 1909 in Tennessee, m: 16
Mar 1929 in Carter, Tennessee

....................... + Jewell Elizabeth Richards b: Abt. 1917, m: 01
Jan 1940 in Bristol, Virginia

.....................4 Joseph Dedrick Overton b: 22 Oct 1904 in
Tennessee, d: 17 Dec 1980 in Harriman, Roane,
Tennessee

....................... + Fannie Elizabeth Jones b: 11 Jan 1910 in
Tennessee, m: 30 Jul 1927 in Roane,
Tennessee, d: 15 Mar 1999 in Kingston, Roane,
Tennessee

.................3 Noah A. Futrell b: 16 Sep 1868 in Morgan,
Tennessee, d: 17 Dec 1929 in Lucas, Ohio

.................. + Mary Jane Cheek b: May 1870 in Tennessee, m:

1898, d: 31 Jan 1929 in Lucas, Ohio

........................4 John L. Futrell b: 07 Jun 1899 in Coalfield,
Morgan, Tennessee, d: 11 Oct 1981 in Toledo,
Lucas, Ohio

........................ + Margaret Mamie LNU b: 1899 in Michigan, d:
14 May 1974 in Lucas, Ohio

........................4 Speedy Albert Futrell b: 07 Jul 1906 in
Coalfield, Morgan, Tennessee, d: 28 Sep 1985 in
Asheville, Buncombe, North Carolina

........................ + Edna S LNU b: 1907, d: 1977

..................3 James Etheldred Futrell b: 16 Mar 1871 in Morgan,
Tennessee, d: 30 Oct 1934 in Coalfield, Morgan,
Tennessee

.................. + Mahala Luiza Adcock b: 12 Apr 1872 in Coalfield,
Tennessee, m: 07 May 1891 in Morgan, Tennessee,
d: 14 Sep 1910 in Coalfield, Morgan, Tennessee

........................4 Albert Harrison Futrell b: 21 Jun 1892 in
Coalfield, Morgan, Tennessee, d: 14 Apr 1965

........................ + Lelah A. Hill b: 14 Jan 1895 in Tennessee, m:
21 Nov 1914 in Morgan, Tennessee, d: 14 Nov
1959

........................4 William Homer Futrell b: 26 Dec 1900 in
Coalfield, Morgan, Tennessee, d: 02 May 1957 in
Mount Vernon, Knox, Ohio

........................ + Beulah Mae Woods b: 13 Feb 1902 in
Tennessee, m: 25 Jan 1922 in Morgan,
Tennessee, d: 24 May 1973 in Lorain, Lorain,
Ohio

.................. + Sarah A (Sally) Farr b: 11 Jun 1894 in Tennessee,
m: 06 Mar 1911 in Morgan, Tennessee

.........................4 Martha Futrell b: 15 Jun 1914 in Tennessee, d:
02 Oct 2005 in Harriman, Roane, Tennessee

......................... + John Burton Humphreys b: 02 Jul 1913 in
Tennessee, m: 04 Mar 1933 in Morgan,
Tennessee, d: Jul 1986 in Harriman, Roane,
Tennessee

.........................4 Vesta Opalee Shipwash b: 20 Sep 1916 in
Tennessee, d: 25 Nov 2009 in Bay Village,
Cuyahoga, Ohio

......................... + Ferry Arnold Shipwash b: 08 Jul 1914 in
Tennessee, m: 03 Jul 1934 in Roane,
Tennessee, d: 12 Aug 1984 in Lorain, Lorain,
Ohio

.........................4 Mary Alice Futrell b: 15 Jul 1924 in Tennessee,
d: 02 Apr 2016 in Clinton, Anderson, Tennessee

......................... + Eblen Major Liles b: 22 Dec 1919 in Tennessee,
m: 15 Apr 1940 in Morgan, Tennessee, d: 19
Feb 1991 in Clinton, Anderson, Tennessee

...................3 William Robert Futrell b: 13 Jun 1873 in Morgan,
Tennessee, d: 29 Mar 1939 in Harriman, Roane,
Tennessee

................... + Margaret Leona Fry b: 17 Feb 1880 in Tennessee,
m: 05 May 1895 in Morgan, Tennessee, d: 05 Aug
1935 in Coalfield, Morgan, Tennessee

.........................4 Leonard Futrell b: 1896 in Morgan, Tennessee,
d: 1896 in Morgan, Tennessee

.........................4 Lonnie Ernest Futrell b: 15 Jun 1897 in Morgan,
Tennessee, d: 14 Mar 1982 in Harriman, Roane,
Tennessee

......................... + Ira Jackson b: Abt. 1901 in Tennessee, m: 09

Jan 1921 in Morgan, Tennessee, d: 09 May

1993 in Harriman, Roane, Tennessee

...................4 Clarence Maynard Futrell b: 18 May 1900 in

Morgan, Tennessee, d: 22 Aug 1971 in Oliver

Springs, Morgan, Tennessee

................... + Sadie Frances Thornton b: 11 Aug 1902 in

Tennessee, m: 19 Sep 1923 in Morgan,

Tennessee, d: 01 Oct 1978

...................4 James Conrad Futrell b: 11 Sep 1903 in

Coalfield, Morgan, Tennessee, d: 25 Sep 1979 in

Oak Ridge, Anderson, Tennessee

................... + Sadie L. Morrison b: 31 Dec 1907 in USA, m: 21

Jul 1927 in Roane, Tennessee, d: 15 Oct 2001

in Oak Ridge, Anderson, Tennessee

...................4 Ella Mae Futrell b: 30 Apr 1906 in Coalfield,

Morgan, Tennessee, d: 02 Jan 1989 in

Harriman, Roane, Tennessee

................... + Henry Elmer Clark b: 19 Jul 1898 in Roane,

Tennessee, m: 22 Jan 1925 in Roane,

Tennessee, d: 30 Apr 1983 in Harriman, Roane,

Tennessee

...................4 Carrie Luvena Futrell b: 13 Mar 1908 in

Morgan, Tennessee, d: 07 May 2004 in Roane,

Tennessee

................... + Paul Aleck Humphreys b: Abt. 1903 in

Tennessee, m: 07 Aug 1927 in Roane,

Tennessee, d: 26 Sep 1956 in Harriman, Roane,

Tennessee

...................4 Lewis Lawrence Futrell b: 18 Dec 1910 in

Morgan, Tennessee, d: 23 Jun 1995 in

Harriman, Roane, Tennessee

...................... + Lassie Phoebe King b: 10 Mar 1916 in Vasper,
        Campbell, Tennessee, m: 03 Jul 1932 in
        Anderson, Tennessee, d: 05 Jul 2000 in Oak
        Ridge Tennessee

......................4 Georgia Evamay Futrell b: 01 Oct 1913 in
        Morgan, Tennessee, d: 15 Oct 1918 in Coalfield,
        Morgan, Tennessee

.................3 Sarah Jane "Sally" Futrell b: 21 May 1878 in
        Morgan, Tennessee, d: 16 Sep 1949 in Kanawha,
        West Virginia

................ + Norris Lucas Bottomlee b: 08 Dec 1867 in
        Tennessee, m: 27 Dec 1897 in Morgan, Tennessee,
        d: 11 Apr 1934

......................4 Walter James Bottomlee b: 07 Jul 1900 in
        Dayton, Rhea, Tennessee, d: 20 Dec 1956 in
        Kanawha, West Virginia

...................... + Artie Lee Frazier b: 01 Nov 1906 in Roxanna,
        Letcher, Kentucky, d: 26 Jan 1994 in Racine,
        Boone, West Virginia

......................4 Leonard Etheldred Bottomlee b: 06 Apr 1902 in
        Coalfield, Morgan, Tennessee, d: 26 Dec 1946 in
        Wyoming, West Virginia

...................... + Josephine Blair b: Abt. 1910 in Kentucky

......................4 Minnie Jane Bottomlee b: 27 Jul 1904 in
        Coalfield, Morgan, Tennessee

...................... + Hibert Dixon b: 01 Jul 1901 in Kentucky, d: 26
        May 1964 in Letcher, Kentucky

......................4 Arnold Norris Bottomlee b: 10 Aug 1906 in
        Morgan, Tennessee, d: 28 Dec 1986 in Beckley,

Raleigh, West Virginia

........................ + J. Pauline Crist b: 24 Jun 1906 in Ansted,
Fayette, West Virginia, m: 06 Nov 1928 in
Fayette, West Virginia, d: 31 Jul 1981 in
Beckley, Raleigh, West Virginia

........................4 Glenn Bottomlee b: Abt. 1909 in Blue Gem,
Morgan, Tennessee, d: 13 May 1911 in Blue
Gem, Morgan, Tennessee

........................4 Viola Mae Bottomlee b: 28 Oct 1911 in
Harriman, Tennessee, d: 02 Sep 1996 in
Premium, Letcher, Kentucky

........................ + Unknown Frazier

.................3 John Albert Futrell b: 29 Nov 1881 in Coalfield,
Morgan, Tennessee, d: 04 Dec 1961

................. + Martha E Bottomlee b: Oct 1891 in Tennessee, m:
26 Dec 1907 in Morgan, Tennessee, d: 28 Dec 1967

........................4 James Franklin Futrell b: 02 Jan 1909 in
Tennessee, d: 29 Apr 1987 in Dayton,
Montgomery, Ohio

........................ + Stella M. Clark b: 10 Aug 1908 in Tennessee,
m: 23 Dec 1926 in Roane, Tennessee, d: 31 Oct
1992 in Dayton, Montgomery, Ohio

........................4 Susan Jane Futrell b: 11 Jun 1911 in Tennessee,
d: 31 Aug 1976

........................ + Samuel B. Jones b: 12 Feb 1889, m: 26 Dec
1926 in Anderson, Tennessee, d: 01 Aug 1963

........................4 Edith Elizabeth Futrell b: 09 Oct 1914 in
Morgan, Tennessee, d: 05 Dec 1999 in
Cincinnati, Hamilton, Ohio

........................ + James Arvel Clark b: 11 Sep 1911 in Coalfield,

Morgan, Tennessee, m: 01 Mar 1932 in

Morgan, Tennessee, d: 14 Jan 2007 in

Loveland, Clermont, Ohio

.............4 John Henry Futrell b: 08 Dec 1917 in

Tennessee, d: 29 Dec 2004 in Marietta,

Greenville, South Carolina

..................... + Mary E. Smith b: 05 May 1921, m: 08 Jul 1940

in Morgan, Tennessee, d: 25 Jan 1991 in

Marietta, Greenville, South Carolina

.............4 Walter Hubert Futrell b: 22 May 1930 in

Tennessee, d: 26 Jan 1995 in Greenville, South

Carolina

..................... + Peggy Manis b: 01 Sep 1937, m: 6 Aug 1954 in

Ringgold, Catoosa, Georgia

.............3 George W. Futrell b: 21 Feb 1885 in Morgan,

Tennessee, d: Bef. 1900

............ + Nellie Byrd b: Oct 1852 in Tennessee, m: 29 Sep 1914

in Morgan, Tennessee

...... + Melinda Martin b: 1819 in Tennessee, m: 20 May 1851 in

Knox, Tennessee

............2 Noah Alexander Futrell b: 16 Mar 1852 in Knox,

Tennessee, d: 22 Jul 1928 in Harriman, Roane,

Tennessee

............ + Sarafina S Edwards b: Abt. 1846 in Tennessee, m: 25

Apr 1869 in Roane, Tennessee, d: Dec 1879

.............3 Etheldred T. Futrell b: 28 Jan 1869 in Tennessee, d:

23 Jan 1952 in Harriman, Roane, Tennessee

............ + Ether Peters b: Abt. 1883 in Tennessee, m: 25 Oct

1900 in Roane, Tennessee, d: 24 Aug 1962

.............4 Eric Brant Futrell b: 02 Jun 1903, d: 28 Jul 1903

..................4 Ellery Ordwell Futrell b: 01 Jul 1904 in
          Harriman, Roane, Tennessee, d: 20 Jan 1978 in
          Oak Ridge, Anderson, Tennessee
.................. + Georgia M. Braden b: Abt. 1909 in Tennessee,
          m: 27 Oct 1928 in Campbell, Tennessee
..................4 Noah A. Futrell b: 25 May 1908 in Tennessee, d:
          29 Nov 1983 in Harriman, Roane, Tennessee
..................4 Elijah W. Futrell b: 25 May 1908 in Tennessee,
          d: 28 May 1981 in Harriman, Roane, Tennessee
..................4 Dora Futrell b: 22 Jun 1913 in Tennessee, d: 28
          Apr 1986 in Harriman, Roane, Tennessee
.................. + Luther Alexander Bagwell b: 21 Apr 1908 in
          Coalfield, Morgan, Tennessee, m: 05 Oct 1928
          in Roane, Tennessee, d: 20 Jun 1984 in
          Chatsworth, Murray, Georgia
................3 Malinda Ann Futrell b: 14 Aug 1871 in Roane,
          Tennessee, d: 12 Aug 1915 in Swan Pond, Roane,
          Tennessee
................ + Alexander Mayton b: 05 Oct 1867 in Roane,
          Tennessee, m: 30 Dec 1894 in Roane, Tennessee, d:
          10 Aug 1921 in Harriman, Roane, Tennessee
..................4 Sarah Elizabeth Mayton b: 05 Sep 1895 in
          Tennessee, d: 17 Oct 1957 in Cleveland,
          Bradley, Tennessee
.................. + Richmond S Baker b: Abt. 1906 in Tennessee,
          m: 16 Dec 1922 in Roane, Tennessee, d: 24 Apr
          1961 in Cleveland, Bradley, Tennessee
..................4 Maggie Carolyn Mayton b: 13 Dec 1897 in Roane
          Tennessee, d: 28 Dec 1944 in Roane, Tennessee
.................. + Floyd Campbell Andrew b: 26 Jul 1892 in

Tennessee, m: 06 Feb 1916 in Roane,

Tennessee, d: 14 May 1985

.......................4 Dora Ellen Mayton b: 22 Nov 1901 in Roane,

Tennessee, d: 05 Apr 1996 in Dayton,

Montgomery, Ohio

....................... + Elder Elden Howard b: 31 Dec 1900 in

Sevierville, Sevier, Tennessee, m: 21 Oct 1922

in Roane, Tennessee, d: 23 Nov 1994 in

Harriman, Roane, Tennessee

.......................4 Andrew Jack Mayton b: 14 Oct 1905 in

Tennessee, d: 09 Nov 1930 in Precinct 1,

Tarrant, Texas

....................... + Teresa McKinney b: 10 Feb 1909 in Roane

Tennessee, m: 25 Oct 1924 in Roane,

Tennessee, d: 10 Aug 1926 in Harriman,

Roane, Tennessee

.......................4 Walter Mayton b: 28 Nov 1908 in Harriman,

Roane, Tennessee, d: 01 Jan 1974 in Cleveland,

Bradley, Tennessee

.......................  + Bonnie M LNU b: 12 Dec 1916, d: 01 Jan 1974

in Cleveland, Bradley, Tennessee

..................3 Elizabeth "Betty" Jane Futrell b: 25 Feb 1875 in

Roane, Tennessee, d: 19 Sep 1948 in Harriman,

Roane, Tennessee

.................. + Frank W. Mullins b: 31 Oct 1870 in Roane,

Tennessee, m: 01 Oct 1893 in Roane, Tennessee, d:

02 Feb 1930 in Harriman, Roane, Tennessee

.......................4 Off Mullins b: 04 Jun 1894 in Roane, Tennessee,

d: 25 Dec 1967 in Caryville, Campbell,

Tennessee

........................ + Myrtle P Adkissin b: 30 Mar 1896 in Tennessee,

          m: 23 Aug 1914 in Roane, Tennessee, d: 15 Jan

          1988 in Harriman, Roane, Tennessee

.......................4 Matilda "Tilda" Melinda Mullins b: 16 Apr 1896

          in Tennessee, d: 15 Sep 1972 in Harriman,

          Roane, Tennessee

........................ + George Washington Taylor b: 03 Apr 1894 in

          Tennessee, m: 23 Nov 1914 in Morgan,

          Tennessee

.......................4 Sarah T. Mullins b: 30 Sep 1899 in Tennessee, d:

          30 Dec 1979 in Sevierville, Sevier, Tennessee

........................ + Virgil Hutsel Peters Sr b: 30 Mar 1894 in

          Harriman, Roane, Tennessee, m: 02 May 1915

          in Roane, Tennessee, d: 20 May 1960

.......................4 Noah T. Mullins b: 23 May 1902 in Harriman,

          Roane, Tennessee, d: 14 Apr 1980 in Harriman,

          Roane, Tennessee

.......................4 Stella May Mullins b: 1904 in Tennessee, d:

          1962

.......................4 William Frank Mullins b: 02 Oct 1907 in

          Harriman, Roane, Tennessee, d: 26 Jan 1947

........................ + Ruth Kate Phillips b: 12 Jun 1911 in Dyllis,

          Roane, Tennessee, d: 29 Sep 1994

.......................4 Versia Mullins b: 31 Mar 1910 in Tennessee, d:

          02 Aug 1981 in Harriman, Roane, Tennessee

........................ + William Howard b: Abt. 1914 in Tennessee, m:

          12 May 1934 in Roane, Tennessee

.......................4 Reese Orey Mullins b: 09 Jun 1914 in

          Tennessee, d: 19 Oct 1978

........................ + Helen Margaret Howard b: 20 Jul 1919 in

Harriman, Roane, Tennessee, m: 08 Apr 1939
in Roane, Tennessee, d: 31 Dec 2003 in
Harriman, Roane, Tennessee

........................ + Bertha Ward b: 27 Sep 1895 in Tennessee, m:
23 May 1942 in Bradley, Tennessee, d: 19 Oct
1969

# Name Index

# P

Patterson
  Josephine, 31
Peters
  Ether, 59, 60, 61, 62, 82
  Virgil Hutsel, 70, 85
Phillips
  Ruth Kate, 72, 85
Poland
  George Thomas, 32, 75

# R

Richards
  Jewell Elizabeth, 34, 76
Robbins
  C.K., 35, 37
  Hester, 37
  James, 37
  Rosa, 37
Ruffin
  Robert, 3, 4

# S

Shipwash
  Ferry Arnold, 41, 78
  Vesta Opalee, 78
Smith
  Mary E., 57, 82

# T

Taylor
  George Washington, 69, 85
Thornton
  Sadie Frances, 44, 79

# U

Underwood
  Morris, 3

# W

Wall
  Isaac, 8
  William Madison, 8
Walls
  Charlotte Charity, 7, 15
  Elizabeth, 17, 22, 24, 31, 35,
    38, 42, 49, 54, 58, 75
  Emily, 37
  John B., 7, 8, 9, 15
  Robert A., 35, 37
  William A., 26
Ward
  Bertha, 69, 86
Wilson
  Willie Frank, 34, 76
Wolf
  Anna, 7, 22
Woods
  Beulah Mae, 39, 77

# Link to Ancestry Data Files

Family tree data supporting the relationships identified in this book are available online at Ancestry.com in the publicly available tree named "The Futrell Family of East Tennessee" under the user name "futrellt".